THE BIG 500
COCKTAIL
PARTY GUIDE

Published in the United Kingdom by

Savisto Limited, 1 Sadler Forster Way, Teesside Industrial Estate, Thornaby, TS17 0JX, U.K.

First printed August 2015

CONTENTS

Introduction

They say the classics never die, and if there was just one word to describe the humble cocktail, it would be endurance. In fact, the very same Martini infamously knocked back heartily by Frank Sinatra at The Savoy in London – four ice cubes swirling in a cascade of gin, freshly squeezed lemon juice and vermouth – can still be readily enjoyed in cocktail lounges the world over.

The origin of the cocktail can be traced back as far as the 1800s and was traditionally comprised of bitters, spirits, sugar and water, but the introduction of liqueurs was the real game changer. With the inclusion of brandy, gin, rum, vodka or whisky came a host of new opportunities for aspiring bartenders to explore and create their own concoctions to appease their patrons, keeping their high-flying consumers queuing deep at the bar.

In 1862, the first known publication to contain cocktail recipes, How to Mix Drinks; or, The Bon Vivant's Companion, was released by the eccentric pioneering American bartender 'Professor' Jerry Thomas. The book was an anthology of the popular drinks of the time, plus a handful of his own creations, which earned him the nickname "the father of American mixology."

With this structure in place, cocktails as they were known evolved from

7

the high-volume sweetened gin that was sunk in abundance by the British and travelled across the Atlantic to take on a more refined public image. By the 1920s, or the années folles, as the French described them, gin joints and cocktail parties became as culturally significant as Art Deco or The Great Gatsby amongst the post-World War hysteria, but it sadly wasn't to last. Black Tuesday – the most destructive New York Stock Exchange crash in Wall Street history – occurred on October 29th 1929, and ushered in The Great Depression with devastating effects on the economy. Over the next decade, the entire western world found themselves destitute and the once revered cocktail faded into obscurity.

It wasn't until the late seventies that the cocktail made its resurgence into popular culture with the flamboyant Blitz Kids of the nightclub scene in London and Birmingham. With heavy endorsement from these shoulder-padded trailblazers of music and fashion, cocktails again returned to prominence, but it was again to be short-lived as New Romanticism gave way to austerity.

In recent years, cocktails have crept back into the forefront of our drinking habits, now armed with centuries of knowledge and, this time, with an eye on longevity. Pulling inspiration from the very same trends that perpetually pushed them into the rear-view, cocktails are now often comprised of a single alcoholic element and just two other key components, usually involving fruit juice of some variety. Old formulas have been revisited to establish fresh and exciting new ideas, while simultaneously representing a throwback to the glory days of the 1920s.

An interesting development in the genetic makeup of the cocktail is the use of flavouring to make the more assertive liquors more palatable; a common practice, at least in America, at a time when alcohol was still outlawed. While no such restrictions apply in modern times, this technique has carried over as a cunning strategy to make cocktails more widely appealing, even to those not particularly enamoured with the taste of alcohol.

There is a fervent debate amongst authors and enthusiasts surrounding the cocktail name and its roots, and no self-respecting book of this genre would be complete without attempting to offer an insight of its own. For every completely plausible theory (such as a possible connection to the coquetier; purportedly the French vessel of the original mixed drinks) there is a downright sobering suggestion; like how the bartenders of yesteryear supposedly combined the dregs from the bottom of the barrel with their punters' leftovers in a ceramic rooster and offered it to their less particular customers at a discounted cost. It could simply be that the name derives from the tail feathers used to garnish early upmarket drinks. It's quite possible that we may never know for sure but, no matter which etymology appeals to you, cocktails seem to, finally, be here to stay.

Ready to get started? Hold your horses - before you dive straight in you should make sure your home is adequately equipped for your cocktail exploits.

Don't worry, you won't need to break the bank to kit out your kitchen, and the Savisto Premium Cocktail Set will cover you for the most part, but, for your convenience, we've thrown together a list of everything you'll need anyway; and offered a quick overview into what makes the essential cocktail kit:

COCKTAIL SHAKER

First thing's first, you'll need a reliable cocktail shaker, and the Savisto Boston Cocktail Shaker will see you through any recipe that calls for one. There are two types of cocktail shakers on the market; the aforementioned Boston shaker and a more simple, traditional shaker. The difference between the two is that a Boston shaker also comes armed with a sixteen ounce mixing glass, which alone is convenient for recipes that simply call for stirring, but bear in mind that you'll need a cocktail strainer to compliment this piece of equipment.

STRAINER

In terms of strainers, you can't go wrong with the Savisto Hawthorne Strainer, which you'll need for recipes that call for shaking or stirring with ice cubes. Not only that, but a halfway good strainer will filter out any pulp, herbs or any other solid that's not welcome in your finest Martini glass after the preparation process is complete.

MEASURES

Next up, you'll need measures, and the Savisto Premium Cocktail Set comes equipped with 25ml and 50ml thimble measures. From there, it's up to you to do the math, for example; a recipe that calls for a 75ml measure will mean a shot from each.

BAR SPOON

For the ideal bar spoon, look no further than the Savisto Twisted Bar Spoon. This long and perforated spoon is ideal for stirring in deep glasses, but was also designed specifically with the intricacies of cocktail making in mind. Its wide and shallow bowl contains the small holes required for floating or layering cocktails that call for it. It might not sound like much, but the effects will blow your guests away.

MUDDLER

A long, sturdy stick with a coarse textured end, the Savisto Wooden Muddler is used to crush, mix, grind and mash ingredients together - usually sugar and fruit - much in the same way a pestle and mortar does. Muddling is an essential step for thoroughly merging flavours into one taste explosion.

BLENDER

We can't even begin to tell you where we'd be without our blender. Making the processes of blitzing herbs, pureeing fruit, crushing ice and mixing liquids timely and efficient, the blender is, to us at least, by far the most essential piece of cocktail equipment. Frozen Daiquiris and Margarita cocktails would simply be impossible to recreate by hand.

GLASSES

You'll need some serious glassware if you're planning to impress your guests. If you want to serve completely authentic drinks, you'll need to serve particular cocktails with their specific counterparts. For example, the Martini goes in the Martini glass. A good rule of thumb to remember is that the stronger the drink, the shorter the glass. We recommend stocking up on a few different glasses, namely a Highball glass, an Old Fashioned glass, a Cocktail glass, a Martini glass, a brandy snifter and a Collins glass. Always remember to handle your glasses by their stem, where possible, to avoid affecting the temperature of your drink and ensuring no undesirable fingerprints are left behind.

UTENSILS

You're likely to find that most kitchen utensils required to create these cocktails are already part of your kitchen setup. You should have a small, dedicated wooden chopping board, however, for cutting fresh fruit. Never use the same board for meat as you run the risk of cross contamination. If you're cutting fruit, it goes without saying that you'll also need a paring knife. It's also best to have a fine grater around for zesting fruit or grating nutmeg.

SPIRITS

The spirits you choose to stock will depend entirely on the cocktails you plan to create, but it's good practice to have a certain few on hand so that, at the very least, you'll always be able to knock something up at a moment's notice. Once your cupboards and shelves are well stocked, you can build from there. Spirits are the most essential items you can stock in your home bar. You will want to keep a bottle of brandy, gin, tequila, vodka and rum available at all times. Bear in mind that, if you're practicing whisky cocktails, one size does not fit all. Each variation has its own distinct characteristics and will drastically affect the outcome of any given recipe. It would be unwise - and incredibly expensive - to keep enough whisky assortments to hand, so we advise you to purchase them on an as-required basis.

LIQUEURS

Liqueurs are where cocktails get their flavour hits. They are made to compliment the chosen base spirit and one bottle will generally last you a long time. You should absolutely always stock a bottle of Amaretto, dry and sweet vermouth, maraschino liqueur and at least one of Cointreau, curacao or triple sec. Depending on the drinks you're planning to make, it's wise to also buy a coffee liqueur, Irish cream liqueur, Benedictine, raspberry liqueur, creme de cacao and Frangelico, but these can be bought as and when you want them.

MIXERS

These non-alcoholic components have gotten themselves a bit of a bad rep thanks to the dire offerings on supermarket shelves, but in truth, the right choice will bring your cocktails to life. There's a good chance you'll already have a lot of items in your fridge and pantry, like cranberry, grapefruit, orange, pineapple and tomato juices, fresh lemons and limes, fresh and frozen fruit, milk and double cream, caster sugar and various sodas. Also keep in mind that you'll be called upon to use ice in the vast majority of the recipes in this book, so always have your ice tray well stocked.

GARNISHES

It's nice to always have this stuff around. Though not essential in cocktail making, presentation is everything and garnishing is your last opportunity to drop a sneaky flavour bomb before you proudly serve up your latest creation. If a recipe calls for you to rim the edge of a cocktail glass, you'll need caster sugar and table salt on hand, and you should always have cocktail sticks stored away. It's worth keeping around plenty of fresh lemons, limes and oranges, as these are the most common garnishes you'll use, but other essentials are olives, mint, nutmeg and maraschino cherries. All other produce should be bought before use to ensure optimal freshness, although you'll probably find things like cinnamon already on your spice rack ready to be used.

Brandy comes from the Dutch word brandewijn, which literally translates to 'burned wine' and is distilled from fermented grapes and other fruits. Like many spirits, it's essential not to skimp on brandy as a low quality bottle will be found wanting.

Cognac, from the French region of the same name, remains the most popular choice for brandy cocktails thanks to its slightly acidic taste and low alcohol volume, but a lot of flavoured brandies (apple, in particular) are starting to make waves as mixologists continue to experiment with different combinations.

B&B
25ml brandy
25ml Benedictine

A simple drink with a simple name, yet unerringly popular, traditionally served neat, the B&B combines brandy with Benedictine – the sweet French herbal liqueur – to create a warming after-dinner delight. Before you begin, warm through a brandy snifter with water, making sure to empty it out before preparing your drink. Simply pour the two ingredients into the snifter, mix together using your Savisto Twisted Bar Spoon and serve.

BALTIMORE BRACER
50ml brandy
50ml absinthe
1 egg white
ice cubes to taste

With a silky texture only achievable with eggs, the Baltimore Bracer packs a powerful punch with full-on flavour. Preparation begins with the chilling of traditional cocktail glass in the freezer. Next, shake all ingredients together in your Savisto Boston Cocktail Shaker until fully combined, ensuring the egg is fully dissolved. Strain into the chilled glass and serve.

BERMUDA HIGHBALL
25 ml brandy
25 ml gin
25 ml dry vermouth
Ginger ale

Offering a quick and easy way to blend three classic cocktail liquors, this drink is created by building the brandy, gin and vermouth in a highball glass and topping up with ginger ale. Garnish with lemon.

BLUE PARADISE
50 ml brandy
50 ml Dubonnet Rouge
10 ml Parfait Amour

If possible, opt for cognac and shake all the ingredients in an iced cocktail shaker before straining into a cocktail glass. Use a lemon peel for garnish.

BOSTON COCKTAIL
50ml apricot brandy
50ml London dry gin
1 tsp grenadine
1 maraschino cherry (optional)
juice of ½ a freshly squeezed lemon
ice cubes

Shake the ingredients together well and strain into a chilled cocktail glass to produce a drink for those with a sweet tooth. Garnish with maraschino cherry.

BOSTON SIDECAR

25ml light rum
25ml triple sec
25ml brandy
juice of a freshly squeezed lime (to taste)
ice cubes to taste

Lying somewhere in the middle of a Daiquiri, Beneath the Sheets and the original Sidecar is the Boston Sidecar; perhaps best known for its sour kick. Make sure to chill your cocktail glasses before serving for an even more luxurious experience. Fill your Savisto Boston Cocktail Shaker with ice, add all the ingredients and shake well. Strain into your chilled glass using the Savisto Hawthorne Strainer and serve.

BRANDY ALEXANDER

25ml brandy
25ml double cream
25ml crème de cacao
ice cubes to taste
freshly ground nutmeg (optional)

This after-dinner accompaniment is perhaps the most popular cream cocktail of all. A significant improvement on the original gin-based Alexander, the hit of chocolate and warming nutmeg in this decadent drink is guaranteed to give you a buzz that will cut through any winter chill. Before serving, chill a cocktail glass in the freezer. Fill your Savisto Boston Cocktail Shaker with ice, brandy, cream and crème de cacao and shake well. Strain into the chilled glass using your Savisto Hawthorne Strainer and dust with ground nutmeg. If you'd prefer, freshly grated dark chocolate works just as well for garnish.

BRANDY COBBLER

75ml brandy
3 tsps caster sugar
2 lime wedges (optional)
1 mint sprig (optional)
club soda
crushed ice

Build the drink in an Old Fashioned glass (filled with crushed ice) and stir well. Top up with club soda, leaving enough room for lime wedges, garnish and serve.

BRANDY COCKTAIL

50ml brandy
2 dashes Angostura bitters
2 dashes Peychaud's bitters
2 tsps curacao
1 lemon twist (optional)
ice cubes

Mix wet ingredients and ice cubes well in your Savisto Boston Cocktail Shaker, strain into a cocktail glass – served neat – and garnish with lemon twist.

BRANDY DAISY

50ml brandy
2 dashes of curacao
2 dashes of rum
2 tsps caster sugar
juice of ½ a freshly squeezed lemon
soda water
ice cubes

Shake brandy, curacao, rum, sugar and lemon juice well with ice cubes in your Savisto Boston Cocktail Shaker. Strain into a cocktail glass with your Savisto Hawthorne Strainer, top up with soda water and serve neat.

BRANDY MILK PUNCH

120ml milk
50ml brandy
1 whole egg
1 tsp caster sugar
ice cubes to taste
freshly ground nutmeg (optional)

This recipe can be traced as far back as the 1600s, where it could be found readily at most soirees. To begin, fill your Savisto Boston Cocktail Shaker with ice, then add all the other ingredients, only holding back the nutmeg for garnish later. Shake extremely well until frothy, then strain into an Old Fashioned glass using your Savisto Hawthorne Strainer. Garnish with nutmeg and serve.

BRANDY SMASH

4 sprigs of fresh mint (plus extra for garnish)
1 tsp caster sugar
50ml brandy
crushed ice to taste
1 wedge of orange (optional)

A classic 'stick' drink not unlike the Mint Julep, which simply means that the ingredients are to be muddled together gently; the Brandy Smash reached the peak of its popularity in the mid-19th century. To begin – using your Savisto Wooden Muddler – carefully grind the sugar and mint together to create a green paste. Throw this rough mixture into an Old Fashioned glass along with the brandy and as much crushed ice as you prefer, and stir well to combine. Garnish with orange wedge, if desired, and additional mint leaves and serve.

BREAST CARESSER

75 ml brandy
50 ml Madeira
25 ml triple sec

For this fruity and rich brandy and Madeira-based treat, simply stir up all of the ingredients in an iced mixing cup. Layer a cocktail glass with crushed ice and pour in the ingredients.

CHAMPAGNE BOWLER

187ml champagne
25ml white wine
3 fresh strawberries (plus extra for garnish)
2 tsps caster sugar
2 tsps Cognac
2 maraschino cherries (optional)
ice cubes

Muddle the strawberries and sugar together in your Savisto Boston Cocktail Shaker to create a sweet paste. Top up with a handful of ice, the cognac and white wine and shake well. Pour the contents into a chilled cocktail glass (rimmed with sugar), top up with champagne and garnish with strawberries and cherries.

CLUB COCKTAIL

50ml brandy
25ml maraschino
25ml pineapple juice
2 dashes of Peychaud's Bitters
ice cubes to taste
1 strawberry (optional)
1 lemon twist (optional)

This tropical cocktail first appeared in W.C. Whitfield's 1939 book Just Cocktails and has remained a popular choice ever since, given its exotic tang is unusually found with brandy drinks. After chilling a cocktail glass in the freezer, fill your Savisto Boston Cocktail Shaker with ice and pour in wet ingredients. Shake well, strain into the chilled glass with your Savisto Hawthorne Strainer, garnish with strawberry and lemon twist and leave to settle for a few minutes before serving.

COFFEE COCKTAIL

50ml brandy
50ml port
1 tsp caster sugar
1 whole free range egg
freshly ground nutmeg (optional)

Bizarrely involving no coffee whatsoever, the Coffee Cocktail involves shaking all the ingredients (bar the nutmeg) particularly well thanks to the inclusion of egg. Strain, serve and garnish with a dusting of nutmeg.

CORPSE REVIVER

50ml brandy
25ml Calvados
25ml sweet vermouth
ice cubes to taste

As the name suggests, the Corpse Reviver comes from a family of 'hair of the dog' cocktails, intended to (at least temporarily) ward off a potential hangover. While most variations have been lost over the years, this recipe – dating back to 1930's The Savoy Cocktail Book by Harry Craddock – survives to this day. After filling your Savisto Boston Cocktail Shaker with ice, add all three alcoholic elements and shake well. Strain into a chilled cocktail glass with your Savisto Hawthorne Strainer and serve.

D'ARTAGNAN

75ml champagne
3 tsps fresh orange juice
1 tsp Armagnac
1 tsp Grand Marnier
1 mint sprig (optional)
½ tsp caster sugar
ice cubes

For this elegant, formal drink, stir together the orange juice, Armagnac, Grand Marnier and sugar. Strain into a flute, top up with champagne and garnish with mint.

DEAUVILLE COCKTAIL

25ml brandy
25ml triple sec
25ml Calvados
juice of a freshly squeezed lemon (to taste)
ice cubes to taste
1 lemon twist (optional)

Originating in New Orleans, the Deauville is a straightforward brandy sour that is easy to follow and even easier to remember. After chilling a traditional cocktail glass, add brandy, triple sec, Calvados and lemon juice to your Savisto Boston Cocktail Shaker filled with ice and shake well. Strain into the chilled cocktail glass using your Savisto Cocktail Shaker and drape lemon twist in the glass before serving.

DELICIOUS SOUR

50 ml peach brandy
50 ml applejack
25 ml fresh lime juice
1 tsp sugar
1 egg white

Create a refreshing party drink with a century-old pedigree by combining all the ingredients in a shaker with no ice first of all and shaking once so the egg blends with the rest of the ingredients. Add ice then shake again before straining into a chilled cocktail glass. Optionally add a dash of soda water at the end.

EGGNOG

50 cl brandy
10 tbsps caster sugar
6 free range egg whites
6 free range egg yolks
2 tsps vanilla extract
½ pint of whole milk
a pinch of salt
freshly ground nutmeg

A winter classic, this creamy eggnog recipe will produce approximately 16 servings. Beat the egg yolks with half the sugar, nutmeg, salt and vanilla extract until thick. Gradually pour in the brandy and milk while still beating, then cover and chill, preferably overnight. Before serving, beat the egg whites and remaining sugar to soft peaks. Pour into the chilled brandy mixture and fold until well mixed. Serve in a mug with a final grating of nutmeg.

EMBASSY

juice of a freshly squeezed lime (to taste)
25ml brandy
25ml golden rum
1 tsp caster sugar
a dash of Angostura bitters
ice cubes to taste
1 wedge of lime (optional)

Famously served at The Embassy in Hollywood and similar in makeup to the Boston Sidecar, this lighter drink draws its inspiration from holiday classics like eggnog but can be enjoyed without the heavy set of its ancestors. To make, first chill your cocktail glass, then fill your Savisto Boston Cocktail Shaker with ice along with the rest of the ingredients, only holding back the lime wedge for garnish later. Shake well, strain and serve.

FANCY BRANDY COCKTAIL

50ml brandy
2 dashes of Peychaud's Bitters
2 dashes of Angostura bitters
1 tsp caster sugar
ice cubes to taste
1 lemon twist (optional)

A drink from a simple time, when you would just order a 'cocktail' with the spirit of your choice and have it made up with bitters, sugar and water for you. The addition of lemon twist as garnish is what technically made a Fancy Brandy Cocktail if you were so inclined. Pour all ingredients into your Savisto Boston Cocktail Shaker, excluding the lemon, and shake well. Strain into a pre-chilled cocktail glass, drape a long ribbon of lemon twist around the glass and serve.

FRENCH 75
juice of a freshly squeezed lemon (to taste)
25ml brandy
1 tsp caster sugar
champagne
ice cubes to taste

Rumour has it this French cocktail gets its name from the 75mm pistol with similar kick. Chill a champagne flute before starting. Fill your Savisto Boston Cocktail Shaker with ice and add brandy, lemon juice and caster sugar. Shake well, strain into the chilled flute, and top up with champagne before serving.

FRIAR TUCK #2
50ml Frangelico
25ml freshly squeezed lemon juice
2 tsps brandy
1 tsp grenadine
cocoa powder (optional)
ice cubes

Shake ingredients together well with ice, strain into an old fashioned glass (rimmed with chocolate) and serve on the rocks.

GINGER ROGERS
25ml apricot brandy
25ml dry gin
25ml dry vermouth
freshly squeezed lemon juice (to taste)
ice cubes

Not unlike its namesake – the famed actress and long-time screen partner of Fred Astaire – the Ginger Rogers is sweet and delicate. Shake all ingredients together well and strain into a chilled cocktail glass.

HARBOUR LIGHT
25ml coffee liqueur
25ml triple sec
2 tsps cognac
1 tsp rum

Float the triple sec onto the coffee liqueur, then the cognac on top of that. Flame the rum on a teaspoon and – carefully – float that into the mix. Put out the fire and enjoy the fruits of your labour.

THE HONEYMOON
50ml applejack
2 tsps Benedictine
2 tsps curacao
2 tsps freshly squeezed lemon juice
ice cubes

Mix all ingredients well in your Savisto Boston Cocktail Shaker, strain into a chilled cocktail glass and serve.

27

HORSE'S NECK

50ml brandy
ginger ale
a few dashes of Angostura bitters (to taste)
1 lemon twist (for garnish)
ice cubes

Build the ingredients in a Collins glass over ice, finishing with the lemon twist draped over the side to resemble – you guessed it – a horse's neck.

MAE WEST

100ml brandy
1 tsp caster sugar
1 egg yolk
ice cubes to taste
cayenne pepper (optional)

Getting its namesake from the sultry American actress of the early 1900s, this spicy cocktail certainly lives up to its name. Fill your Savisto Boston Cocktail Shaker with ice and shake well with the brandy, sugar and yolk until fully combined. Strain into a traditional Highball glass filled with ice using your Savisto Hawthorne Strainer, dust with a generous pinch of cayenne pepper and enjoy.

METROPOLITAN

50ml brandy
25ml sweet vermouth
2 dashes of Angostura bitters
1 tsp caster sugar
ice cubes to taste

The Metropolitan talks the talk, and it most certainly holds its own against other classic cocktails of its ilk. While there are other cocktails with the same namesake, this brandy recipe is considered to be the oldest, though not the most popular, to take the mantle. To recreate this sophisticated nightcap, prepare a cocktail glass by placing it in the freezer to chill for a few hours. When ready, fill your Savisto Boston Cocktail Shaker with ice and add all other ingredients. Shake well, strain into the chilled glass using your Savisto Hawthorne Strainer and serve.

MILLENNIUM

50ml orange juice
25ml gin
2 tsps cherry brandy
ginger ale
ice cubes

Shake together the orange juice, gin, brandy and ice cubes, then strain into a chilled cocktail glass. Top up with ginger ale and serve.

MILLIONAIRE

25ml apricot brandy
25ml golden rum
25ml sloe gin
1 dash of grenadine
juice of a freshly squeezed lime
ice cubes

Fill your Savisto Boston Cocktail Shaker with ice cubes and shake well with the rest of the ingredients. Strain into a chilled cocktail glass using your Savisto Hawthorne strainer and serve immediately.

MORNING GLORY

25ml cognac
25ml whisky
2 dashes of Angostura bitters
1 tsp absinthe
1 tsp caster sugar
1 tsp curacao
club soda
ice cubes

Stir all ingredients (sans soda) well in a mixing glass filled with ice, strain into a traditional Old Fashioned glass, top up with club soda and serve.

NIGHTCAP
25ml brandy
25ml absinthe
25ml curacao
1 egg yolk
ice cubes to taste

A great addition to your repertoire thanks to its straightforward ingredients, the Nightcap is a soothing option at the end of a hard day's work. After chilling a standard cocktail glass, add all ingredients to your Savisto Boston Cocktail Shaker and dry shake. Add ice, shake vigorously again and strain before serving. A smooth consistency is vital for this intriguing and tantalising little drink.

OAK ROOM SPECIAL
50ml brandy
50ml cherry brandy
50ml crème de cacao
1 free range egg white

Fill your Savisto Boston Cocktail Shaker with ice cubes and all four ingredients, shaking well to ensure the egg is fully dissolved. Strain into a chilled cocktail glass and serve.

PISCO SOUR

50ml pisco
25ml freshly squeezed lemon juice
3 dashes of Angostura bitters
2 tsps caster sugar
1 egg white
1 mint sprig (optional)
ice cubes

Combine all ingredients, excluding bitters, into your Savisto Boston Cocktail Shaker with ice and shake well. Strain into a chilled cocktail glass, add bitters, garnish with mint leaves and serve.

PORTO FLIP

50ml port
1 free range egg yolk
1 tsp brandy
freshly ground nutmeg (optional)

Shake ingredients well, strain into a chilled cocktail glass and finish with a pinch of nutmeg.

SANGRIA

1.5 litres red wine
1 litre club soda
75ml curacao
50ml brandy
4 tsps caster sugar
juice of a freshly squeezed lemon
juice of a freshly squeezed orange
ice cubes
fresh lemon slices (optional)
fresh orange slices (optional)
fresh peach slices (optional)

Chill all ingredients overnight, then mix the wine, curacao, brandy, juice and sugar together. Strain into a large punch bowl with plenty of ice, top up with club soda and garnish with fruit slices. Serves 24.

SARATOGA BRACE UP

50ml brandy
2 dashes of absinthe
2 dashes of Angostura bitters
1 tsp caster sugar
1 whole egg
juice of a freshly squeezed lemon (to taste)
club soda
ice cubes to taste

Originally appearing in 'Professor' Jerry Thomas' definitive Bartender's Guide, the Saratogo Brace Up is another recipe to embrace the magic of absinthe in a mixed drink. Fill your Savisto Boston Cocktail Shaker with ice and then add the absinthe, bitters, brandy, egg, lemon and sugar. Shake until smooth and strain into a traditional Highball glass. Top up with sofa water and serve on the rocks, if you'd prefer, but the original recipe doesn't call for it.

SIDECAR

50ml cognac
25ml Cointreau
2 tsps freshly squeezed lemon juice
ice cubes
1 flamed lemon twist (optional)

If you use a decent cognac with this recipe, the combination of lemon juice and cointreau should really bring out its delicate flavours. Fill your Savisto Boston Cocktail Shaker with ice and shake the cognac, Cointreau and lemon juice well. Strain into a chilled cocktail glass, garnish with flamed lemon twist and serve.

SNOWBALL

50ml brandy
1 tsp caster sugar
1 whole egg
ginger ale
ice cubes to taste
1 lemon wedge (optional)
1 maraschino cherry (optional)

Not unlike a Gin Fizz, the Snowball is the perfect go-to recipe at any time of the year. In the winter, it offers comfort and an air of grandeur to life your spirit, while with the summer comes an instant refreshment. Fill your Savisto Cocktail Shaker with ice along with the brandy, caster sugar and egg. Shake well; making sure the egg is fully combined with the other ingredients, before straining into a Collins glass filled with ice. Top up with ginger ale, dunk a red cherry into the glass, and garnish with the lemon wedge.

STAR COCKTAIL
50ml apple brandy
50ml sweet vermouth
3 dashes of Angostura bitters
2 tsps caster sugar

Stir all ingredients together in your Savisto Boston Mixing Glass, strain into a chilled cocktail glass and serve.

TOM & JERRY
25ml brandy
25ml dark rum
1 tsp caster sugar
1 whole egg
hot milk
freshly ground nutmeg (optional)
1 star anise (optional)

Traditionally served at Christmas in a mug rather than your standard cocktail glass, this warming treat is guaranteed to keep the winter chill at bay. Separate the egg and beat the white until stiff. In another bowl, mix the yolk and sugar together, then put a teaspoon of this mixture into a mug along with the brandy and rum. Stir well then fold in some of the egg white. Top up with hot milk and remaining egg white to create a peak, then garnish with nutmeg and star anise.

VIEUX CARRE

25ml cognac
25ml sweet vermouth
25ml whiskey
a dash of Angostura bitters
a dash of Peychaud's bitters
½ a tsp of Benedictine
ice cubes
2 maraschino cherries (optional)
1 wedge of orange (optional)

Stir ingredients well in your Savisto Boston Mixing Glass, strain over ice in an old fashioned glass and garnish with cherries and orange.

WEEP NO MORE

50ml brandy
50ml Dubonnet Rouge
¼ teaspoon maraschino
juice of a freshly squeezed lime (to taste)
ice cubes to taste

Another classic from the Just Cocktails book by W.C. Whitfield and was a clear favourite in the early 1900s, but stands the test of time even today. To recreate this cheerful pick-me-up, first fill your Savisto Boston Cocktail Shaker with ice then throw in the other ingredients and shake well. Strain into a previously chilled cocktail glass using your Savisto Hawthorne Strainer and serve immediately for a quick, easy and instantaneous morale booster.

WISCONSIN OLD FASHIONED

50ml brandy
2 dashes of Angostura bitters
2 orange slices (plus extra for garnish)
2 fresh red cherries (plus extra for garnish)
1 tsp caster sugar
lemon-lime soda
ice cubes to taste

Traditionally a before-dinner drink popular in the Midwest, the brandy Old Fashioned has spent most of its life being upstaged by its whiskey-based cousin. This recipe, however, looks to reclaim the Old Fashioned mantle for brandy lovers around the world, with an ambitious array of deep flavours. Tip the caster sugar into the bottom of a classic Old Fashioned glass and soak it with a splash of bitters and soda. Add the orange slices and red cherries and muddle using your Savisto Wooden Muddler. Fill the glass with ice cubes, add the brandy and stir well before topping up with more soda. Garnish with additional orange and cherry before serving.

Gin was originally created to treat kidney disease and became mass produced in England when King William III banned imported French liquor. It gets its name from the French translation for the juniper berry, where it gets its flavour.

There are a number of great gins with their own qualities, so use your discretion when choosing which gin to compliment the other flavours in your cocktail. Your best bets are London Dry and Plymouth gin.

20th CENTURY

75ml gin
25ml Lillet Blanc
25ml white crème de cacao
1 dash of fresh lemon juice
ice cubes

Pour all ingredients into a cocktail shaker filled with ice. Shake well and strain into a chilled cocktail glass.

ABBEY COCKTAIL

50ml gin
50ml fresh orange juice
2 dashes of Angostura bitters
ice cubes

The more refined cousin of the Orange Blossom, the Abbey Cocktail originates from The Savoy in London and is traditionally to be enjoyed at brunch. Add all ingredients to your Savisto Boston Cocktail Shaker and shake well before straining into a chilled cocktail glass. This tangy drink packs a punch and is the perfect accompaniment to a fried breakfast if you're suffering the effects of the night before.

ADMIRAL BENBOW

75ml Plymouth gin
50ml dry vermouth
25ml freshly squeezed lime juice
ice cubes
1 maraschino cherry (optional)

Pour all ingredients into a mixing glass with several ice cubes. Stir well before straining into a low-ball glass filled with ice. Garnish with the cherry to serve.

ALEXANDER

25 ml gin
25 ml crème de cacao
75 ml light cream

For a smooth and easy gin tipple, shake all the ingredients with ice in a cocktail shaker. Strain into a cocktail glass and optionally garnish with nutmeg.

ALLIES COCKTAIL

50ml dry vermouth
50ml gin
2 dashes of Kümmel
ice cubes

Pour the ingredients over ice cubes in a cocktail shaker. Stir well and strain into a chilled cocktail glass.

ANGEL FACE

50 ml gin
25 ml apricot brandy
25 ml apple brandy

'Autumn in a glass' is one way of describing this combination of gin, apricot and apple brandy. To create it, stir up all the ingredients with a handful of ice cubes before straining into a chilled cocktail glass.

AVIATION

50ml gin
1 tsp maraschino
1 dash of crème de violette
juice of a freshly squeezed lemon (to taste)
ice cubes to taste
1 flamed lemon twist (optional)

First printed in the 1916 book Recipes for Mixed Drinks, the Aviation cocktail has stood the test of time and remains a popular choice throughout gin joints around the world. Fill your Savisto Boston Cocktail Shaker with ice and pour in all wet ingredients. Shake well then strain into a chilled cocktail glass using your Savisto Hawthorne Strainer. This drink is traditionally garnished with flamed lemon peel, but you can just use a plain lemon twist if you aren't comfortable with flaming your own.

BARNUM WAS RIGHT

75 ml gin
25 ml apricot brandy
4 dashes angostura bitters
4 dashes lemon juice

P.T. Barnum was famous for coining the phrase, "There's a sucker born every minute". Quite how this particular concoction came to be named in honour of him is now something of a mystery. Nonetheless, the result is a drink that stays just on the right side of being too sweet. It's made by shaking up the ingredients with cracked ice and straining into a chilled cocktail glass. Add a lemon twist for garnish.

BEBBO

75 ml gin
50 ml lemon juice
30 ml honey
Dash orange juice

It sounds almost too sweet but works a treat. Heat the honey in a microwave until it turns into a liquid. Before you add the ice into your cocktail shaker, pour in all the ingredients until they combine. Add ice and shake again until well chilled. Strain into a cocktail glass and optionally add a cherry before serving.

BEES KNEES
50ml gin
2 tsps freshly squeezed lime juice
1 tsp runny honey
ice cubes

A simple survivor of the Prohibition era, rumour has it that this sweet treat was cleverly used to disguise the alcohol at the time of its embargo. While no such law exists today, the Bees Knees has stuck around, and, in truth, we're glad that it did. To recreate, fill your Savisto Boston Cocktail Shaker with ice along with the other ingredients and shake well, taking care to make sure the honey is well mixed. Strain into a chilled cocktail glass using your Savisto Hawthorne Strainer and serve.

BELLES OF ST. MARY'S
50 ml gin
25 ml apricot brandy
25 ml triple sec
2 tsp lemon juice

To recreate this regal and ancient gin tipple, add all the ingredients to an iced shaker and shake well before straining into a chilled cocktail glass.

BILTMORE

50ml gin
25ml sweet vermouth
1 piece of fresh pineapple
1 dash of maraschino liqueur
ice cubes
1 maraschino hazelnut (optional)

Soak a hazelnut in maraschino liqueur for at least 2 (and ideally 24) hours. Muddle the pineapple in a mixing glass before adding gin, vermouth and maraschino and fill with ice. Shake well and strain into a cocktail glass. Add the marinated liqueur as a garnish.

THE BRAMBLE

50ml gin
25ml fresh lime juice
25ml creme de mure liqueur
2 tsps caster sugar
ice cubes
a few mint leaves (optional)
fresh blackberries (optional)

This is one of our favourites and comes from the great Soho cocktail revival of the 80s. There are a number of different variations of Dick Bradsell's brainchild but this is the version we like the most. Fill your Savisto Boston Cocktail Shaker with ice along with the gin, lime juice and sugar and shake well to mix. Fill a Highball glass with ice cubes and strain in the mixture with your Savisto Hawthorne Strainer. Throw in some mint leaves and a handful of fresh blackberries, allow to settle and then drizzle over the creme de mure slowly to create a gorgeous gradient effect.

THE BRONX

50ml gin
25ml orange juice
2 tsps sweet vermouth
2 tsps dry vermouth
ice cubes
1 orange slice (optional)

Another disciple of the Martini, this product of early 1900s New York takes the successful formula for a Perfect Martini and adds a hit of orange juice to the already popular mix. You'll find that this isn't as dry as many Martinis can be, so it's a great alternative if that isn't your preference. Fill your Savisto Boston Cocktail Shaker with ice along with the wet ingredients and shake well. Strain into a chilled cocktail glass with your Savisto Hawthorne Strainer, garnish with orange and serve.

CAROLI

75 ml gin
25 ml apricot brandy
2 dashes orange bitters

Half-fill your mixing glass with crushed ice. Pour in all of the ingredients and stir well before straining into a cocktail glass.

CLARIDGE

50 ml gin
50 ml dry vermouth
Dash apricot brandy
Dash triple sec

Stir up all the ingredients in a mixing glass along with a handful of ice. Strain into a cocktail glass and optionally add an orange peel to garnish.

CLOVER CLUB COCKTAIL

50ml gin
1 tsp raspberry liqueur
1 tsp caster sugar
1 egg white
juice of a freshly squeezed lemon (to taste)
ice cubes to taste
3 fresh raspberries (optional)

Reportedly a creation of the Bellevue-Stratford Hotel in Philadelphia, the Clover Club Cocktail is every mixologist's dream thanks to its sustained relevance despite evolving trends. Though more modern variations often call for the inclusion grenadine rather than raspberry liqueur, any bartender worth his salt will agree that it is no substitute for this frothy and fruity delight. Add all ingredients, excluding raspberries, to your Savisto Boston Cocktail Shaker and fill with ice. Shake well; ensuring the egg is well combined with the rest of the mixture, and strain into a chilled cocktail glass using your Savisto Hawthorne Strainer. Garnish with fresh raspberries on a cocktail stick to evoke an even greater feeling of luxury.

COMMUNIST

50 ml gin
50 ml fresh orange juice
25 ml cherry brandy
50 ml fresh lemon juice

This cocktail may be over 70 years old – but it's still as delicious as ever!
Simply shake up all the ingredients in an iced cocktail shaker and strain into
a cocktail glass.

COSTA DEL SOL

50 ml gin
25 ml Cointreau
25 ml apricot brandy

Shake all of the ingredients together in an iced shaker and strain into an
old-fashioned glass. Throw in a couple of ice cubes before serving.

CORPSE REVIVER #2

25ml gin
25ml Lillet Blanc
25ml Cointreau
1 dash of absinthe
juice of a freshly squeezed lime (to taste)
ice cubes to taste
1 maraschino cherry (optional)

As was the case with the original brandy-based Corpse Reviver, this
descendent is designed to revive the poor souls who may have endured a
skinful too many. If you need help to fend off the morning after, simply fill
your Savisto Boston Cocktail Shaker with ice, add all wet ingredients and

shake well. Strain into a chilled cocktail glass using your Savisto Hawthorne Strainer and plop in the cherry. Hangover be gone!

DIRTY MARTINI

75ml gin
2 tsps dry vermouth
2 tsps olive brine
ice cubes
an odd number of olives (optional)

Don't let the name fool you, the Dirty Martini is perfectly hygienic. A variation of the classic Martini, the 'dirty' aspect comes from the addition of olive brine, which tastes a lot better than it sounds. You'll want to experiment with a quantity that suits your own taste, but what we've outlined is a good jumping off point. Use more or less as desired. Pour the wet ingredients and ice cubes into your Savisto Boston Mixing Glass and stir. Strain into a chilled cocktail glass and garnish with three or five olives (an even number brings bad luck with it) before serving.

DOLOMINT

25ml gin
25ml Galliano
25ml freshly squeezed lime juice
ginger ale
ice cubes
a few sprigs of fresh mint (optional)

A natural evolution of the Gin Buck, the addition of Galliano really gives this cocktail a fantastic character. With hints of vanilla and aniseed, the Dolomint is as refreshing as it is sweet and sour. Fill a traditional Highball glass with ice and pour in the gin, Galliano and lime juice. Stir well using your Savisto Twisted Bar Spoon, top up with ginger ale and toss in a couple of sprigs of fresh mint.

DUBONNET COCKTAIL

50ml gin
25ml Dubonnet Rouge
ice cubes
1 lemon twist (optional)

The cocktail of choice for Queen Elizabeth II and her mother, the Dubonnet (or Zaza) has faded into obscurity, but we think it's important that, for all the glitz and glamour of the modern cocktail, that we don't forget our roots. Combine the gin and Dubonnet Rouge with ice in your Savisto Boston Mixing Glass and stir well. Strain into a chilled cocktail glass using your Savisto Hawthorne Strainer and garnish with lemon twist to serve.

EMERSON

50ml gin
25ml sweet vermouth
2 tsps maraschino liqueur
2 tsps lemon juice
ice cubes

An alternate take on the Martinez (the Martini's predecessor), the Emerson takes an already successful formula and adds a kick of lemon juice that is a welcome change. Pour all ingredients into your Savisto Boston Cocktail Shaker and shake well. In a chilled cocktail glass, strain this mixture with your Savisto Hawthorne Strainer and serve.

FAT FACE

50 ml gin
25 ml apricot brandy
10 ml Grenadine
1 egg white

Place all the ingredients in a shaker (before adding the ice) and stir to combine. Add a handful of ice cubes, shake well and strain into a lowball glass with a couple of ice cubes.

FLORODORA

50ml gin
25ml raspberry liqueur
juice of a freshly squeezed lime (to taste)
ginger ale
ice cubes to taste
1 lemon wedge (optional)

While not quite as popular as it used to be, you'll still find the Florodora (or, alternatively, Floradora) in most reputable cocktail guides suited to breath-taking summertime refreshments. In a classic Highball glass filled with ice, add gin, raspberry liqueur and lime juice before topping up the glass with ginger ale. Stir lightly and garnish with lime wedge before serving.

FOGHORN

75ml gin
50ml freshly squeezed lime juice
ginger ale
1 lime wedge (optional)

Pour gin and lime juice into a low-ball glass filled with ice. Stir well. Top with ginger ale, stir gently and garnish with a wedge of lime.

FORD

50 ml gin
50 ml dry vermouth
3 dashes Benedictine
3 dashes orange bitters

For this herby sitrus mix, stir the ingredients together in an iced cocktail shaker before straining into a cocktail glass. Optionally garnish with orange peel.

G&T

50ml gin
tonic water
ice cubes to taste
lime wedge (optional)

While the classic Gin & Tonic might seem as though it's simple enough, it's important to remember that it's only ever going to be as good as its ingredients. Since this is a cocktail that relies heavily on its simplicity, make sure to buy the best quality tonic water and gin you can afford to really appreciate this time-honoured refreshment. Fill a traditional Highball glass with ice and add the gin and tonic. Stir well, garnish with the lemon wedge, and serve.

GIMLET
50ml gin
50ml lime cordial
ice cubes
1 lime twist (optional)

If simple gin sours are your bag, this sweet and tart drink will leave you green with envy. The beauty of this cocktail is in its simplistic nature, as it really allows a quality gin's taste to shine through, so we recommend using a good London Dry for this one. In your Savisto Boston Mixing Glass, stir the gin and lime cordial well with ice cubes, then strain into a chilled cocktail glass using your Savisto Hawthorne Strainer. Garnish with lime twist and serve.

GIN & IT
50ml gin
25ml sweet vermouth

You may be worried about what "it" constitutes, but it simply stands for Italian vermouth, and what you see if exactly what you get with this descendant of the Martini. Combine the gin and "it" directly in a cocktail glass, stir with your Savisto Twisted Bar Spoon and serve neat.

GIN & SIN

25ml gin
25ml freshly squeezed lemon juice
25ml fresh orange juice
a dash of grenadine
ice cubes

The 'sin' in this Martini alternative probably comes from the sweet fruit juices that were considered extravagant at one time. Truthfully, it isn't very sinful, so you can enjoy this guilt-free. Pour all ingredients into your Savisto Boston Cocktail Shaker and shake well. Strain into a chilled cocktail glass using your Savisto Hawthorne Strainer and serve.

GIN BUCK

50ml gin
ginger ale
ice cubes
1 lemon wedge (optional)

A simple and refreshing mixed drink, the Gin Buck was the inspiration behind the more modern Dragonfly, Foghorn and Leap Frog cocktails. Fill a traditional Highball glass with ice, pour in the gin and top up with ginger ale. Stir, garnish with a lemon wedge and serve. Quick, easy and deeply satisfying before or after a meal.

GIN FIZZ

50ml gin
1 tsp caster sugar
lime juice
soda water
1 lime twist (optional)

The Fizz family is still an extremely popular choice throughout the world, though they have adapted with time. This recipe doesn't stray too far from the original gin sour that was first noted in Jerry Thomas' Bartender's Guide. Shake the gin, sugar and lime juice together with ice in your Savisto Boston Cocktail Shaker and strain into a chilled Highball glass. Top up with soda water, garnish with lime twist and serve.

GIN MARTINI

75ml gin
2 tsps
a dash of Angostura bitters
ice cubes
3 green olives (optional)

Pour gin and vermouth into a mixing glass filled with ice cubes. Stir for 30 seconds and strain into a chilled cocktail glass. Add a dash of bitters if desired and garnish with olive or lemon.

GIN RICKEY
50ml gin
club soda
juice of a freshly squeezed lime (to taste)
ice cubes to taste
1 lime wedge (optional)

In a traditional Highball glass, throw in enough ice to fill along with the gin and lime juice. Top up the glass with club soda and garnish with lime wedge to serve. This simple, refreshing drink makes the perfect alternative to the classic Gin and Tonic was allegedly invented by Colonel Joe Rickey in 1883 after asking for lime to accompany his regular Mornin's Morning.

GIN ROOT
50ml gin
25ml beetroot juice
25ml freshly squeezed lemon juice
a sprig of fresh mint
ice cubes

In your Savisto Boston Cocktail Shaker, add the gin, beetroot juice, lemon juice, mint and ice cubes and shake well until mixed thoroughly. Strain into a champagne flute and serve.

GIN SLING

50ml gin
25ml freshly squeezed lemon juice
25ml sweet vermouth
2 tsps caster sugar
1 dash of Angostura bitters
soda water
ice cubes
1 lemon slice (optional)

This sweet and sour thirst-quenching combination is one of the most tried and tested gin cocktails in circulation. You'll still find it in cocktail lounges around the world and, while the recipe may alter slightly, the taste remains largely the same. Pour all wet ingredients - excluding the soda - into your Savisto Boston Cocktail Shaker with ice, shake well and strain into a chilled collins glass. Top up with soda water, garnish with lemon slice and serve on the rocks for an unparalleled refreshment.

GOLDEN DAWN

50ml apricot brandy
50ml calvados
50ml gin
50ml orange juice
ice cubes

Pour all ingredients into a cocktail shaker filled with ice. Shake the contents well before straining into a chilled cocktail glass.

GREAT DANE

50ml gin
2 tsps caster sugar
2 tsps freshly squeezed lime juice
a dash of free range egg white
ice cubes

Shake ingredients well with ice until egg is well combined, then strain into a cocktail glass.

HANKY PANKY

50 ml gin
50 ml sweet vermouth
2 dashes Fernet Branca

Fernet Branca is one of those love it or hate it slightly bitter liqueurs that needs to be experienced at least once. Stir the ingredients in a a cocktail shaker filled with ice. Strain into a cocktail glass and garnish with a strip of orange peel.

HI-HO COCKTAIL

50ml gin
25ml white port
4 dashes of orange bitters
ice cubes
1 lemon twist (optional)

Pour ingredients into ice-filled cocktail shaker. Shake well before straining into a chilled cocktail glass. Garnish with a lemon twist.

HONOLULU COCKTAIL

50ml gin
1 tsp caster sugar (plus extra for rimming)
1 dash of Angostura bitters
splash of pineapple juice
splash of orange juice
ice cubes to taste
juice of a freshly squeezed lemon (to taste)
1 lemon twist (optional)

Whether you're lounging on a beach in the sun or taking shelter from the miserable weather, this sweet, fruity treat will leave you feeling as though you've escaped to the Northern Tropic. To begin, rim the outside of a cocktail glass with lemon and caster sugar, then pour all wet ingredients (and sugar) into your Savisto Boston Cocktail Shaker with ice. Shake well, strain into the prepared cocktail glass using your Savisto Hawthorne Strainer and garnish with lemon twist for a real summertime buzz.

INCOME TAX

50ml gin
25ml fresh orange juice
1 tsp dry vermouth
1 tsp sweet vermouth
1 dash of Angostura bitters
ice cubes
1 orange twist (optional)

Whether you're drowning your sorrows or celebrating an unexpected rebate, the Income Tax is an extremely sweet mixture of fine liqueurs and tangy orange juice. Combine all wet ingredients with ice cubes in your Savisto Boston Cocktail Shaker and shake well before straining into a chilled cocktail glass using your Savisto Hawthorne Strainer. Garnish with orange peel and serve.

JOHNNY WEISSMULLER

50ml gin
50ml lemon juice
50ml light rum
1 tsp caster sugar
1 dash of grenadine
ice cubes

Pour all ingredients into a cocktail shaker with ice cubes. Shake well before straining into a chilled cocktail glass.

THE JOURNALIST

50ml gin
2 tsps dry vermouth
2 tsps sweet vermouth
2 dashes of curacao
2 dashes of freshly squeezed lemon juice
1 dash of Angostura bitters
ice cubes

A cocktail dating back to the early 1900s which provided inspiration for the many late night musings of a columnist's typewriter, the Journalist is a fresh take on the Perfect Martini, combining the classic formula of dry and sweet vermouth with a fruity citrus hit. Fill your Savisto Boston Mixing Glass with ice, pour in all other ingredients and stir well with your Savisto Twisted Bar Spoon. Using your Savisto Hawthorne Strainer, strain the mixture into a chilled cocktail glass and serve immediately to stimulate your creativity.

JUPITER

75 ml gin
50 ml dry vermouth
10 ml Parfait Amour
10 ml orange juice

Combining gin with a hint of blueberries, this drink first appeared in a 1923 cocktail compendium – although its precise origins are unknown. Combine all ingredients with ice in a cocktail shaker. Shake well before straining into a cocktail glass.

LAST WORD

25ml gin
25ml Chartreuse
25ml lime juice
25ml maraschino liqueur
ice cubes

Based on its ingredients of four equal ingredients, one may suspect that this cocktail could be a mishmash of flavours, but rest assured, The Last Word is one of tastiest drinks to survive the Prohibition era. Fill your Savisto Boston Cocktail Shaker with ice, pour in all ingredients and shake well until smooth. Strain into a chilled cocktail glass using your Savisto Hawthorne Strainer and serve immediately.

LEAP YEAR

50ml gin
25ml Grand Marnier
25ml sweet vermouth
2 tsps freshly squeezed lemon juice
ice cubes
1 lemon twist (optional)

Pour ingredients into an ice-filled cocktail shaker. Stir well before straining into a chilled cocktail glass. Garnish with a lemon twist.

LUCIEN GAUDIN

50 ml gin
25 ml Cointreau
25 ml Campari
25 ml dry vermouth
Orange twist to garnish

Named after a 19th Century French fencing champion, this Negroni-esque creation is made by stirring the ingredients in a mixing glass with ice before straining into a cocktail glass and garnishing with an orange twist.

MARTINEZ

50ml gin
25ml sweet vermouth
1 tsp maraschino
1 dash of Angostura bitters
ice cubes to taste
1 lemon twist (optional)

The ancestor of arguably the most popular cocktail of all time – the Martini – this variation brings a sweeter element to the gin and vermouth combination than its successor. Fill your Savisto Boston Mixing Glass with ice, then add all wet ingredients and stir well. Strain into a chilled cocktail glass using your Savisto Hawthorne Strainer and garnish with lemon twist.

MARTINI

75ml gin
25ml dry vermouth
a dash of Angostura bitters
ice cubes to taste
an odd number of olives (optional)

There may not be another cocktail carrying the heavy name value of the classic Martini. Contrary to the preference of a certain fictional Secret Service agent, we definitely prefer our Martinis stirred, as we find shaking bruises the gin and waters down the naturally complementary flavours of gin and vermouth. Fill your Savisto Boston Mixing Glass with ice cubes, pour in wet ingredients and stir gently for approximately half a minute. Strain into a chilled cocktail glass using your Savisto Hawthorne Strainer and add a dash of Angostura bitters to complete this beloved, humble little drink. For garnish, use either one or three olives (skewered on a cocktail stick) as superstition dictates that an even number will bring bad luck, and you don't want that now, do you?

MIAMI ICED TEA

25ml cranberry juice
25ml sour mix
2 tsps gin
2 tsps light rum
2 tsps peach schnapps
2 tsps triple sec
2 tsps vodka
lemon & lime soda
ice cubes

Build all the ingredients in a collins glass, top up with soda and stir well.

MILLION DOLLAR COCKTAIL

120ml pineapple juice
50ml gin
1 tsp dry vermouth
1 tsp sweet vermouth
a dash of Angostura bitters
a dash of free range egg white
ice cubes

Pour the gin and vermouths into a cocktail shaker with ice cubes. Add the pineapple juice, egg white and Angostura bitters. Shake vigorously to froth up the egg white and strain into a chilled highball glass.

MINNEHAHA

50ml gin
25ml dry vermouth
25ml sweet vermouth
1 tsp fresh orange juice
ice cubes

Pour all ingredients into your Savisto Boston Cocktail Shaker and shake well before straining into a chilled cocktail glass using your Savisto Hawthorne Strainer. Taking its name from Minnehaha Falls in Georgia, this dry cocktail takes the successful formula of The Bronx and flips it on its head.

MONKEY GLAND

50ml gin
25ml orange juice
1 tsp grenadine
1 dash of absinthe
ice cubes to taste
1 flamed orange twist (optional)

A fantastic drink with a sordid history, Harry McElhone claims to have invented this drink, and his explanation for its name is of disturbing significance. In his 1922 book, Harry's ABC of Mixing Cocktails, McElhone explains that the name was inspired by the experiments of Serge Voronoff who, before the days of Viagra, treated impotence by grafting monkey testicle tissue onto human testicles. If that hasn't put you off trying this cocktail for yourself (and trust us, it shouldn't), then pour all wet ingredients into your Savisto Boston Cocktail Shaker, fill with ice and shake well. Strain into a chilled cocktail glass using your Savisto Hawthorne Strainer, garnish with flamed orange peel and serve immediately.

NAPOLEON

50ml gin
2 tsps Dubonnet Rouge
2 tsps Grand Mariner
ice cubes
1 orange twist (optional)

An exciting aperitif in its own right, the Napoleon combines Dubonnet Rouge - a classic spiced red wine - with Grand Mariner which, along with a high quality gin, makes the perfect before dinner drink. Mix all wet ingredients with ice cubes in your Savisto Boston Cocktail Shaker and shake well. Strain into a chilled cocktail glass with your Savisto Hawthorne Strainer, garnish with orange twist and serve.

NEGRONI

50ml gin
50ml Campari
50ml sweet vermouth
ice cubes to taste
1 orange twist (optional)

A proud aperitif thanks to the addition of Campari, the Negroni is one of a number of cocktails designed to stimulate the appetite before dinner and, in truth, it's probably one of the best. Presumably created for and named after Count Camillo Negroni at the Café Casoni, the sweet vermouth in this enjoyable and cleansing little drink neutralizes the Campari, so don't worry if you aren't usually too fond of its bitter taste. Fill an Old Fashioned glass with ice and wet ingredients. Stir well, throw in the orange twist, and serve.

NEW ORLEANS FIZZ

50ml double cream
50ml gin
2 dashes of fleurs d'orange
2 tsps caster sugar
2 tsps freshly squeezed lemon juice
2 tsps freshly squeezed lime juice
1 free range egg white
club soda
ice cubes

Place all the ingredients except the club soda into a cocktail shaker with ice cubes. Shake vigorously to ensure the egg and cream are well mixed. Strain into an ice-filled highball glass and top with club soda.

NO SLEEP

50ml gin
2 tsps freshly squeezed lemon juice
a handful of fresh raspberries (plus extra for garnish)
a pinch of freshly ground black pepper
pear juice
ice cubes

Muddle the raspberries with the lemon juice in the bottom of your Savisto Boston Cocktail Shaker, then add the gin, pepper and a handful of ice cubes. Shake well, strain into a chilled old fashioned glass and garnish with additional raspberries.

OBITUARY

50ml gin
1 tsp absinthe
1 tsp dry vermouth
cracked ice to taste

As the name suggests, the Obituary is not for the faint hearted. Not entirely unlike a classic Martini, this fierce drink differs with the inclusion of the green fairy. One thing to keep in mind is that the better the gin, the better the taste, and this cocktail deserves quality. Fill your Savisto Boston Mixing Glass with cracked ice and all three ingredients. Stir well then strain into a chilled cocktail glass using your Savisto Hawthorne Strainer and serve.

ORANGE BLOSSOM

25ml gin
25ml fresh orange juice
25ml sweet vermouth
ice cubes

This is a fantastic crowd pleaser to add to your repertoire thanks to its equal three-part ingredient list. There are two versions of the Orange Blossom, at least according to The Old Waldorf-Astoria Bar Book, but we prefer sweeter version served neat. In your Savisto Boston Mixing Glass, combine the three ingredients with ice cubes and stir well with your Savisto Twisted Bar Spoon. Strain into a chilled cocktail glass using your Savisto Hawthorne Strainer and serve.

PARADISE

75ml fresh orange juice
50ml gin
25ml apricot brandy
ice cubes

Pour ingredients into a cocktail shaker with ice. Shake well before straining into a well-chilled cocktail glass.

PARK AVENUE

50ml gin
1 tsp dry vermouth
1 tsp sweet vermouth
a splash of pineapple juice
ice cubes to taste
1 orange twist (optional)

Essentially a Perfect Martini with added pineapple, the Park Avenue is a perfect alternative for those with an aversion to the dry Martini but fancy a similar sort of drink. Combine all wet ingredients with ice in your Savisto Boston Cocktail Shaker and shake well. Strain into a chilled cocktail glass using your Savisto Hawthorne Strainer and leave to settle before serving.

PERFECT MARTINI

50ml gin
2 tsps sweet vermouth
2 tsps dry vermouth
ice cubes

A 'perfect' cocktail is a celebration of vermouth. In cocktail terms, it simply means equal parts of both dry and sweet vermouth, which makes for a refreshing change of pace from the usual Martini fare. Fill your Savisto Boston Mixing Glass with above ingredients and stir well with your Savisto Twisted Bar Spoon. Strain into a chilled cocktail glass using your Savisto Hawthorne Strainer and serve. You can, if you wish, garnish with olives, but we think this simple combination speaks volumes for itself.

PEGU CLUB COCKTAIL
50ml gin
25ml orange liqueur
2 dashes Angostura bitters
ice cubes to taste
juice of a freshly squeezed lime (to taste)
1 lime twist (optional)

After seemingly fading into obscurity after the second World War, the Pegu Club Cocktail is undergoing a resurgence of sorts in recent times, with many cocktail outlets opting to add it to their menus again. Fill your Savisto Boston Cocktail Shaker with ice with all other ingredients (holding back the lime peel for garnish later), shake well and strain into a chilled cocktail glass using your Savisto Hawthorne Strainer. Garnish and serve.

PINK GIN
50ml gin
4 dashes of Angostura bitters

A simple combination of gin and bitters, you might think that this humble mixed drink isn't worth your time, but you'll be pleasantly surprised by this straightforward aperitif. Shake the two ingredients together in your Savisto Boston Cocktail Shaker with ice and strain into a chilled cocktail glass using your Savisto Hawthorne Strainer. That's it. No fuss, no hassle, just a delightful, appetising little drink.

PINK LADY

50ml gin
25ml applejack
2 dashes of grenadine
1 egg white
juice of a freshly squeezed lemon (to taste)
ice cubes to taste
1 maraschino cherry (optional)

The key to this blushing, delicate drink is the addition of grenadine, which gives it the pink hue from where it gets its name. Fill your Savisto Boston Cocktail Shaker with ice and all other ingredients, shake vigorously until the egg is fully combined, then strain into a chilled cocktail glass using your Savisto Hawthorne Strainer. Garnish with maraschino cherry and serve.

POLAR COCKTAIL

75ml gin
75ml maraschino liqueur
1 free range egg white
juice of ½ a freshly squeezed lemon
ice cubes

Pour all ingredients into a cocktail shaker filled with ice. Shake vigorously to ensure the egg is fully mixed before straining into a frozen cocktail glass.

RAMOS GIN FIZZ

50ml gin
50ml double cream
2 dashes of Fleur d'Orange
2 tsp caster sugar
1 egg white
club soda
juice of a freshly squeezed lemon (to taste)
juice of a freshly squeezed lime (to taste)
ice cubes to taste

Accredited to Henry C. Ramos, who came up with this cocktail in late 1800s New Orleans, the Ramos Fizz is an incredibly popular choice even today. First, fill your Savisto Boston Cocktail shaker with ice along with all other ingredients, except club soda. Shake well (a good rule of thumb is to shake until it hurts your arm) until the milk and egg are fully combined with the rest of the ingredients. Fill a standard Highball glass with ice and strain the mixture into it using your Savisto Hawthorne Strainer. Top up with club soda and serve to invoke the true spirit of the 1915 Mardi Gras.

ROGUE ALASKAN

25ml freshly squeezed lemon juice
25ml gin
1 tsp caster sugar
a dash of absinthe
a dash of Angostura bitters
champagne
lemon peel (optional)

Stir ingredients (bar champagne and lemon peel) well with ice, then pour over fresh ice in a chilled lowball glass. Top up with champagne, garnish with lemon peel and serve.

ROSE COCKTAIL

50ml gin
2 tsps Kirsch
2 tsps dry vermouth

Shake all ingredients together well and strain into a chilled cocktail glass.

SAKETINI

75ml gin
2 tsps sake
3 green olives (optional)

Mix the gin and sake in a mixing glass filled with ice before stirring well. Strain into a chilled cocktail glass and garnish with an olive.

SALTY DOG

50ml gin
grapefruit juice
table salt
1 wedge of fresh lime (optional)

Rim a Collins glass with lime juice and salt, fill with ice cubes and pour in the gin. Top up with grapefruit juice, garnish with lime wedge and serve.

SINGAPORE SLING

50ml club soda
50ml gin
25ml freshly squeezed lime juice
2 tsps caster sugar
2 tsps cherry brandy
ice cubes
1 lemon slice (optional)
1 maraschino cherry (optional)

Shake gin, lemon juice and syrup in a cocktail shaker. Strain into highball glass with ice cubes. Pour in club soda, float cherry brandy on top by pouring it over the back of a bar spoon. Garnish with lemon and cherry on a cocktail skewer.

SLOE SCREW

50ml sloe gin
orange juice
ice cubes
1 wedge of fresh orange (optional)

Pour the gin over ice in a traditional highball glass and top up with orange juice. Garnish with orange segment and serve.

SMOKY MARTINI

75ml gin
a dash of Scotch
ice cubes
1 lemon twist (optional)

Pour ingredients into a mixing glass filled with ice. Stir and strain into a chilled cocktail glass and garnish with a lemon twist.

THANKSGIVING

50ml apricot brandy
50ml dry vermouth
50ml gin
1 dash of lemon juice
ice cubes
1 maraschino cherry (optional)

Pour all ingredients into a cocktail shaker with ice and shake well. Strain into a chilled cocktail glass and garnish with the cherry.

TOM COLLINS

50ml gin
2 tsps caster sugar
juice of a freshly squeezed lemon (to taste)
club soda
ice cubes to taste
1 lemon slice (optional)

A refreshing gin sour that bites back, the Tom Collins was destined to be enjoyed under the sun with good company. Finding the balance of sweet and sour here can be difficult, but you want enough lemon juice for a slightly sour kick against the sugar. Pour the gin, lemon juice and sugar into a Collins glass and stir well. Taste, adding more lemon juice if you prefer, then top up with club soda, ice and garnish.

TUXEDO

50ml gin
50ml dry vermouth
2 dashes bitters
¼ tsp absinthe
¼ tsp maraschino liqueur
ice cubes to taste
1 lime wedge (optional)
1 maraschino cherry (optional)

If you were to attend any number of formal social events, you're increasingly likely to find a well-suited high roller clutching this elegant anise drink gracefully. Begin by filling a mixing glass with ice along with all wet ingredients and stir. In a chilled cocktail glass, strain using your Savisto Hawthorne Strainer, garnish with the lime wedge and cherry and serve for an immediate glimpse into how the other half live.

VESPER MARTINI

75ml gin
25ml vodka
2 tsps Lillet Blanc
1 lemon twist (optional)

Shake all ingredients together. Pour and a large thin slice of lemon peel for garnish.

WHITE LADY

50ml gin
25ml Cointreau
25ml lemon juice
ice cubes
1 maraschino cherry (optional)

A forgotten relic of the Sidecar family, we believe the White Lady is just too good to allow it to completely fade into obscurity. Fill your Savisto Boston Cocktail Shaker with ice and pour in all wet ingredients. Shake well then, with your Savisto Hawthorne Strainer, strain into a chilled cocktail glass.

WILL ROGERS

75ml gin
50ml dry vermouth
50ml fresh orange juice
4 dashes of curacao

Pour all ingredients into a cocktail shaker with ice cubes and shake well. Strain into a chilled cocktail glass.

YALE COCKTAIL

50ml gin
2 tsps dry vermouth
1 tsp blue curacao
1 dash of bitters
ice cubes
1 lime twist (optional)

A cocktail to throw your senses a curveball, the Yale Cocktail looks alluring and tastes sublime. As clear blue as the Mediterranean sea, the refreshing citrus kick makes this drink perfect for your summer rotation. Pour all wet ingredients into your Savisto Boston Mixing Glass with ice cubes and stir well. In a chilled cocktail glass, strain this mixture using your Savisto Hawthorne Strainer, garnish with lime twist and serve.

Rum has become a rather broad term as each different variety can be so much different than the last. Originating in South America and the Caribbean, your options include dark rum, light rum, golden rum and various spiced rums, which became popular in the 20th century.

What sets rum apart from the other spirits is the use of sugarcane in the fermenting process. This is turned into molasses and gives rum a much sweeter complexion than other spirits, making it a pleasant change of pace from other cocktail bases.

ALOHA
15 ml dark rum
10 ml dry vermouth
10 ml cognac
10 ml gin
15 ml lime juice
30 ml soda water

Promising a strong and instant Hawaiian kick, this drink is created by shaking up all the ingredients in an iced shaker before straining into a cocktail glass. Garnish with a slice of lime.

ANEJO HIGHBALL
50ml Anejo rum
50ml ginger beer
2 dashes of Angostura bitters
2 tsps curacao
2 tsps freshly squeezed lime juice
ice cubes
1 wedge of lime (optional)

In a highball glass, build the ingredients over ice. Garnish with lime and serve.

BACARDI SPECIAL

75 ml Bacardi rum
25 ml gin
Juice of 1 lime
Dash of Grenadine
1 tsp sugar

For a delicious way to combine gin and Bacardi, try this for size: shake all the ingredients apart from the rum in an iced shaker. Add the rum and shake again. Strain into a cocktail glass.

BAHAMA MAMA

120ml pineapple juice
2 tsps coconut liqueur
2 tsps dark rum
1 tsp Bacardi 151 rum
1 tsp coffee liqueur
juice of ½ a freshly squeezed lemon
1 maraschino cherry (optional)
1 pineapple wedge (optional)

Shake ingredients together and pour over cracked ice. Garnish and serve.

BANANA DAIQUIRI

50ml freshly squeezed lime juice
50ml light rum
2 tsps triple sec
1 banana
1 tsp caster sugar
ice cubes
1 lime twist (optional)
1 pineapple wedge (optional)
1 fresh raspberry (optional)

Blend ingredients with ice cubes until smooth and serve in a chilled hurricane glass with fruit garnish.

BEACHCOMBER

50ml light rum
25ml freshly squeezed lime juice
25ml triple sec
2 dashes of maraschino liqueur
1 tsp caster sugar
ice cubes
1 orange twist (optional)

Shake ingredients well with ice cubes, strain into a chilled cocktail glass and drop in the orange twist before serving.

BELLADONNA

25ml dark rum
25ml light rum
25ml orange juice
25ml cranberry juice
25ml pineapple juice
ice cubes

The Belladonna gets its name from a poisonous plant, but there's nothing toxic about this combination of rums and juices that originated in tiki-style bars. An easy recipe to remember, Belladonna takes one measurement of two rums and three juices, making this a quick cocktail to throw together when the mood takes you. Simply add all liquids to your Savisto Boston Cocktail Shaker with ice cubes, shake well, and strain into a collins glass filled with ice using your Savisto Hawthorne Strainer.

BETWEEN THE SHEETS

25ml brandy
25ml light rum
25ml triple sec
2 tsps lemon juice
ice cubes
lemon twist for garnish

A simple drink related to the Sidecar, Between the Sheets adds a delightful twist with the addition of triple sec and lemon juice. Multiple theories exist as to the origin of the drink's name, but even without the provocative title its creation during the Prohibition era was sure to cause minor scandal. Easy to drink and even easier to mix, simply combine all ingredients into your Savisto Boston Cocktail Shaker with ice cubes, shake, and strain into a chilled glass using your Savisto Hawthorne Strainer. Garnish if desired.

BLUE HAWAII

25ml rum
25ml blue curaçao
25ml creme de coconut
25ml pineapple juice
1 maraschino cherry for garnish
1 pineapple wedge for garnish
ice cubes

Though it's easy to imagine a cocktail being inspired by the Elvis Presley movie of the same name, the Blue Hawaii was actually created four years prior to the film's release. The result of an experiment to create a signature cocktail featuring the very vivid blue colour of Curaçao liqueur, the Blue Hawaii is otherwise very similar to the Piña Colada, with both drinks having a frozen option for those who like things a bit colder. Mix the rum, Curaçao, creme de coconut, and pineapple juice in your mixing glass with ice cubes, taking care to stir well. Strain into a collins glass filled with ice cubes - using your Savisto Hawthorne Strainer - and garnish with the pineapple, cherries, or other tropical fruits.

BOSSA NOVA

50 ml dark rum
25 ml apricot brandy
25 ml Galliano
25 ml lemon juice
Pineapple juice to top

Shake all the ingredients apart from the pineapple juice in an ice-filled shaker. Strain into a collins glass lined with a handful of ice cubes. Top with pineapple juice and stir well. Optionally garnish with a chunk of pineapple.

CABLE CAR

50ml freshly squeezed lemon juice
50ml spiced rum
25ml orange curacao
2 tsps caster sugar
ice cubes
orange peel (optional)

A classic rum sour, the Cable Car's inspiration came from the tram tracks not far from its place of invention. Shake the ingredients well using your Savisto Boston Cocktail Shaker and strain into a chilled cocktail glass. Garnish with orange peel and serve immediately.

CAIPIRINHA

50ml rum
4 wedges of fresh lime
2 tsps caster sugar
crushed ice

Muddle the lime wedges and sugar at the bottom of a chilled old fashioned glass. Fill with crushed ice, pour in the rum and stir gently. You'll want to try and keep the sugar from sinking to the bottom of the glass, so give your glass a whirl every so often to keep things moving.

COMMODORE

75ml rum
1 egg white
½ tsp caster sugar
1 dash of lemon juice
1 dash of grenadine
1 dash of raspberry liqueur
ice cubes

The perfect cocktail for those with a sweet tooth, the Commodore combines sugars, syrups and flavoured liqueurs to create a beverage slightly thicker than your average cocktail, thanks in part to the unusual presence of egg white. The dash of lemon juice helps to cut through the sweetness, but make no mistake; this is not a cocktail that evenly balances tart against sweet. Combine all ingredients with ice in your Savisto Boston Cocktail Shaker, shake well, and strain into a chilled cocktail glass using your Savisto Hawthorne Strainer. Serve immediately.

DAIQUIRI

50ml light rum
25ml lime juice
1 tsp caster sugar
ice cubes

Though the Frozen Daiquiri has taken over on beach resorts around the world, the classic Daiquiri involves no crushed ice and only three simple ingredients. Rum is the key, with lime juice and a sweetener - usually sugar or a syrup - balancing out each ingredients' respective tartness or sweetness. Pour the rum, lime juice, and sugar over ice into your Savisto Boston Cocktail Shaker, shake well, and then strain into a chilled glass using your Savisto Hawthorne Strainer. Add additional lime juice or sugar to taste.

DARK & STORMY

75ml ginger beer
50ml black rum
ice cubes
1 wedge of lemon (optional)

Combine ingredients in a highball glass, garnish and serve on the rocks.

DULCE DE LECHE

25ml Bacardi rum
2 tsps condensed milk
2 tsps dark chocolate liqueur
1 tsp caster sugar
ice cubes

Shake ingredients together and strain into a chilled cocktail glass.

ELECTRIC ICED TEA

25ml freshly squeezed lemon juice
2 tsps blue curacao
2 tsps gin
2 tsps light rum
2 tsps tequila
2 tsps vodka
lemon & lime soda
ice cubes
1 slice of lemon (optional)

Build ingredients in a collins glass over ice, finishing by floating the blue curacao over the rest of the drink.

FLORIDATA DAIQUIRI

75 ml rum
10 ml maraschino liqueur
Juice of half a lime
1 tsp sugar

This drink originates from La Florida Bar, Havana – Hemingway's favourite haunt. To recreate thirties glamour in a glass, shake up all the ingredients in an iced shaker. Strain into a champagne saucer or cocktail glass before serving.

FOGCUTTER

50 ml white rum
25 ml gin
25 ml brandy
15 ml sweet and sour mix
2 dashes simple syrup
Dash sherry brandy

Created by one of the 1930s pioneers of 'tiki' bars and drinks, this cocktail is created by adding all the ingredients with ice in a cocktail shaker and shaking well. Strain into a cocktail glass, float the cherry brandy on top and serve.

FROZEN PIÑA COLADA

175ml fresh pineapple juice
50ml coconut cream
50ml white rum
25ml double cream
ice cubes
1 pineapple wedge (optional)
1 maraschino cherry (optional)

Though not the kindest on the waistline; this tropical iced Pina Colada is a treat for your taste buds. Blend ingredients together with as much ice as you'd like – experiment to find the perfect consistency for you – ideally, just enough to create a slush. Pour into a hurricane glass, garnish and serve immediately.

FISH HOUSE PUNCH

750ml dark rum
450ml Cognac
225ml peach brandy
225ml lemon juice
1 cup caster sugar
1 block of ice

Every summer soiree needs a punch, and Fish House Punch has proved to be a staple at gatherings for many decades. Though the misleading name suggests an unpalatable presence of seafood, this punch gets its name from the private Fish House Club in Philadelphia where it originated. Place the block of ice in the bottom of a large punch bowl, add all ingredients and stir well until the sugar is dissolved. Serve with punch glasses and let your guests help themselves. This recipe will yield approximately ten servings.

HOT BUTTERED RUM

1 small slice softened butter
1 tsp brown sugar
cinnamon, nutmeg or allspice
vanilla extract
2 ml dark rum
hot water

Not necessarily a beverage for the heart health conscious, Hot Buttered Rum nonetheless provides a delicious combination of flavours reminiscent of the best holiday baking. Festive spices and warm butter are a treat when combined with the warmth of the vanilla and rum, providing a perfect antidote to the winter chills. Place the brown sugar, butter, and preferred combination of spices in the bottom of an Irish coffee glass, and mix well. Pour in rum and hot water and stir.

HOT TODDY

50ml rum
1 tbsp honey
juice from ¼ of a lemon
1 cup hot water
1 tea bag

A favourite on cold winter nights, the Hot Toddy is a flexible beverage whose only real requirement is that it's warm and smooth going down. More often utilising whiskey as its base ingredient, we find rum completely transforms this drink and changes its complexion for the better. Flavours can be adjusted dramatically through your choice of brandy, whiskey, or rum combined with green or black teas - so experiment to find your preferred concoction! Coat the bottom of a mug or glass with the honey, and then add the rum and lemon juice. Separately, steep the tea bag in a cup of hot water and then pour over the honey, rum, and lemon juice. Stir well and serve while still hot.

HURRICANE

50ml dark rum
50ml light rum
50ml fresh passion fruit juice
25ml fresh orange juice
2 tsps caster sugar
2 tsps grenadine
juice of ½ a freshly squeezed lime
ice cubes
1 maraschino cherry (optional)
1 slice of orange (optional)

Fill your Savisto Boston Cocktail Shaker with ice and shake ingredients together. Strain into a hurricane glass and garnish with cherry and orange.

JEAN HARLOW

50ml light rum
50ml sweet vermouth
ice cubes
1 lemon twist (optional)

Named after Hollywood's original sex symbol, who reportedly preferred her martini sweet and with rum. Shake the ingredients together with ice, strain into a cocktail glass, garnish with lemon twist and serve neat.

KNICKERBOCKER

75ml rum
2 tsps raspberry liqueur
2 tsps orange curacao
25ml fresh lemon juice
ice cubes
1 lemon wedge (optional)
fresh raspberries (optional)

Though its popularity peaked in the 19th century, the Knickerbocker is an understated, fruity drink fabulous for garnishing with fresh raspberries when in season. Pour the rum, raspberry syrup, orange curacao, lemon juice and ice into a glass and stir well. Strain into a chilled cocktail glass, garnish with lemon or raspberries, and serve.

LONG BEACH ICED TEA

25ml cranberry juice
25ml freshly squeezed lemon juice
2 tsps gin
2 tsps light rum
2 tsps tequila
2 tsps triple sec
2 tsps vodka
1 slice of orange (optional)

Stir ingredients together in a collins glass over ice and garnish with orange.

LOUNGE LIZARD

50ml dark rum
2 tsps amaretto
cola
ice cubes
1 maraschino cherry (optional)

Mix the rum and amaretto over ice in a traditional collins glass and top up with cola. Garnish with cherry and serve.

MADISON AVENUE

50ml white rum
25ml Cointreau
2 tsps lime juice
1 dash of orange bitters
mint leaves
ice cubes
1 sprig of mint for garnish
lime slice for garnish

A distant cousin of the more common Mojito, the Madison Avenue was a 1930s creation that emerged from the Weylin Bar on - you guessed it - Madison Avenue in New York City. The Madison Avenue keeps the Mojito's rum, limes, and mint, but takes things up a notch with the addition of citrus flavours in the form of both orange bitters and Cointreau. With the orange flavours balancing the mint, the Madison Avenue is a delightfully refreshing cocktail. Add the rum, Cointreau, lime juice, orange bitters, and a few mint leaves to a cocktail shaker and shake well. Strain into an old fashioned glass over ice, and serve with either a slice of lime or a sprig of mint as garnish.

MAI TAI

25ml dark rum
25ml light rum
2 tsps amaretto
2 tsps freshly squeezed lime juice
2 tsps orange curacao
ice cubes
1 wedge of fresh orange (optional)

Shake the light rum, amaretto, lime juice and curacao well with ice to combine then strain into a chilled old fashioned glass over fresh ice. Add the shot of dark rum, garnish with orange segment and serve (with a cocktail umbrella for authenticity).

MARY PICKFORD

75ml light rum
75ml pineapple juice
1 teaspoon grenadine
1 teaspoon maraschino cherry juice
ice cubes

Oscar winning silent movie star Mary Pickford was one of Hollywood's first megastars and it's only natural that she have a cocktail named after her. With it's cherry and pineapple juices plus syrupy grenadine, the Mary Pickford packs a pink punch perfect for a summer's day. Pour all ingredients in your Savisto Boston Cocktail Shaker over ice, shake well, and strain into a cocktail glass using your Savisto Hawthorne Strainer.

MOJITO

2 tsps sugar
6-8 mint leaves
club soda
1 lime, halved
75ml light rum
ice cubes (crushed, if preferred)
1 mint sprig for garnish

Though slightly more involved than its cousin the Daiquiri, what the Mojito increases in prep time it more than makes up for with freshness. Mint is the true star of this cocktail, with the herb providing a lovely cooling sensation perfect for pairing with a hot summer day. In a Highball glass, muddle the sugar, mint leaves and a small amount of club soda - with your Savisto Wooden Muddler - until the sugar is dissolved. Squeeze the juice from both lime halves into the glass; slice half the lime and add to the glass if desired. Add the rum and stir well to combine. Fill the glass with the ice cubes, and add the remainder of the club soda. Garnish with mint if desired.

NAKED LADY

50 ml rum
50 ml sweet vermouth
10 ml apricot brandy
10 ml lemon juice
Dash Grenadine

Pour all the ingredients into an iced shaker and shake thoroughly. Strain into a cocktail glass.

NAVY GROG

25ml white rum
25ml demerara rum
25ml dark rum
25ml lime juice
25ml white grapefruit juice
25ml runny honey
club soda
ice cubes
1 orange slice or maraschino cherry

The name might conjure up Victorian-era ships circumnavigating the globe, but Navy Grog as it exists today is a far cry from its maritime namesake. History may have found sailors drinking from barrels filled with any combination of liquors and other liquid ingredients, but today's Navy Grogs have a more cohesive list of ingredients, though that list might change from recipe to recipe. Combine all rums, juices and syrup plus ice in your Savisto Boston Cocktail Shaker and shake well. Strain into a collins glass filled with ice, using your Savisto Hawthorne Strainer, and top up with club soda, and garnish with the orange slice and cherry.

PAINKILLER

50ml rum
25ml coconut cream
25ml freshly squeezed lemon juice
pineapple juice
ice cubes
a handful of fresh strawberries (optional)

Shake the rum, coconut cream and lemon juice with ice. Strain into a chilled highball glass over fresh ice, top up with pineapple juice and garnish with strawberries.

PIÑA COLADA
75ml light rum
75ml pineapple juice
50ml cream of coconut
1 pineapple wedge for garnish
1 maraschino cherry for garnish
ice cubes

Like with the Daiquiri, the Piña Colada has suffered in recent years owing to the popularity of its frozen sibling. Even without pulverized ice, the Piña Colada is still enjoyed by many and it's no wonder: with pineapple and coconut flavours, it makes for a wonderful, tropical, refreshing treat. Pour rum, juice, and cream of coconut into your Savisto Boston Cocktail Shaker over ice, shake well, and strain into a cocktail glass using your Savisto Hawthorne Strainer. Garnish with pineapple, maraschino cherries, or other tropical fruit.

PLANTER'S PUNCH
50ml dark rum
50ml tropical fruit juice
1 tsp grenadine
club soda
ice cubes
1 maraschino cherry (optional)
1 orange twist (optional)

In a mixing glass, stir the rum, juice and grenadine over ice. Strain into a highball glass on the rocks, top up with club soda and garnish with fruit.

RUM & COKE

50ml rum
cola
ice cubes
1 wedge of lime (optional)

We're not going to insult your intelligence here, but this simple classic is absolutely deserving of its place amongst other heavyweight cocktail recipes. Pour the rum over ice in a traditional highball glass, top up with cola and, if you're feeling adventurous, squeeze a little lime into the mix.

RUMPKIN SPICE

50g pumpkin puree
50ml fresh apple juice
50ml rum
2 tsps free range egg white
1 tsp caster sugar
ginger beer
juice of a freshly squeezed orange
ice cubes
piece of fresh ginger (optional)

Shake all ingredients well (sans ginger beer) and strain into a chilled tall glass over ice. Top up with ginger beer, garnish with ginger and serve.

RUM RUNNER

50ml golden rum
2 tsps freshly squeezed lemon juice
2 tsps fresh pineapple juice
2 tsps strawberry liqueur
a dash of grenadine
orange juice
ice cubes
1 lemon twist (optional)
1 pineapple wedge (optional)
½ a strawberry (optional)

Shake the rum, lemon juice, pineapple juice, strawberry liqueur and grenadine with the ice cubes in your Savisto Boston Cocktail Shaker. Strain into a chilled hurricane glass, top up with orange juice and garnish with assorted fruits.

SCORPION

50ml fresh orange juice
25ml brandy
25ml dark rum
25ml light rum
1 tsp triple sec
juice of ½ a freshly squeezed lime
ice cubes
1 wedge of lime (optional)

Shake ingredients well with ice in your Savisto Boston Cocktail Shaker and strain into a highball glass. Garnish with lime wedge and serve on the rocks.

STRAWBERRY DAIQUIRI

100g fresh strawberries (plus extra for garnish)
50ml light rum
25ml freshly squeezed lime juice
2 tsps triple sec
1 tsp caster sugar
ice cubes

Blend ingredients until smooth, pour into a chilled margarita glass and garnish with additional sliced strawberries.

THE THIRD RAIL

25ml applejack
25ml rum
25ml Cognac
1 dash of absinthe
ice cubes

As electrifying and potentially fatal as its namesake, the Third Rail is not a cocktail to be trifled with thanks to the presence of absinthe. Though only a dash of the Green Fairy is included in this drink, it's enough to create a powerful combination best served with care. Combine all ingredients into your Savisto Boston Cocktail Shaker with ice cubes, shake well, and strain into a chilled cocktail glass using your Savisto Hawthorne Strainer.

ZOMBIE

50ml fresh orange juice
50ml fresh pineapple juice
25ml Bacardi 151
25ml dark rum
25ml light rum
25ml orange curacao
2 dashes of Angostura bitters
2 tsps freshly squeezed lemon juice
2 tsps freshly squeezed lime juice
1 tsp grenadine
ice cubes
1 pineapple wedge (optional)

Approach with caution; the Zombie gets its name from the state it can leave those of a weaker disposition. Shake the ingredients well with ice and strain into a highball glass over fresh ice. Garnish with pineapple wedge and serve.

5. Tequila

Tequila's history dates all the way back 2,000 years, not as a vessel to harbour morning regrets, but rather as a prominent part of Mexico's heritage and religious rituals.

Since then, tequila has evolved to become one of the highest quality spirits on the market, thanks to its constantly improving industry regulations. The highly potent liquor is made with the sweet nectar of the agave plant, which contributes massively to its signature taste.

APPLE MARGARITA

25ml fresh apple juice

25ml apple liqueur

25ml tequila

2 tsps sour mix

ice cubes

caster sugar

ground cinnamon

2 watermelon cubes (optional)

1 lemon twist (optional)

If you're a fan of the Frozen Margarita found later in this chapter, you're sure to love this variation that combines that ice blast with the refreshing tang of apple. As always, we recommend making your own sour mix (it's super easy and the balance is perfect) but premade can be used reasonably. Pour all wet ingredients into a blender with ice cubes and blitz until smooth. Keep adding ice, if required, and pulse until the mixture resembles slush. Chill a margarita glass, rim with a combination of apple liqueur, cinnamon and sugar and pour in the contents of the blender. Place watermelon cubes and lemon on a cocktail skewer, garnish and serve.

BLOODY MARIA

50ml tequila

3 dashes of Tabasco sauce

3 dashes of Worcestershire sauce

1 dash of freshly squeezed lime juice

1 pinch of celery salt

1 pinch of freshly ground black pepper

1 tsp Dijon mustard

1 tsp horseradish

tomato juice

ice cubes

1 celery stalk (optional)

1 cherry tomato (optional)

1 lemon slice (optional)

This sublime sibling of the Bloody Mary swaps vodka for tequila to give a unique and exciting flavour that is arguably an improvement on the original. The biggest difference between the two comes from the strength of the alcohol; where vodka tends to get lost amongst all the other flavours, the tequila cuts through the spice just enough to shine. Fill a traditional Highball glass with ice cubes and slowly build up the rest of the ingredients, before finally topping up with tomato juice. Stir well, making sure to combine every flavour, and garnish with celery stalk, cherry tomato and lemon slice. As history dictates, this is a drink to be savoured when you're suffering.

BLUE MARGARITA
50ml tequila
25ml blue curacao
25ml freshly squeezed lime juice
ice cubes
table salt
1 maraschino cherry (optional)
1 orange twist (optional)

Pour wet ingredients into your Savisto Boston Cocktail Shaker with ice and shake well. Meanwhile, rim a margarita glass with table salt, then pour in the contents of your shaker. Garnish with cherry and orange twist and serve. This cocktail takes the classic Margarita and turns it on its head with a stunning electric blue that will knock your senses for six, thanks to blue curacao replacing the usual triple sec.

BRAVE BULL ·

50ml tequila
25ml kahlua

Essentially a Mexican-inspired Black Russian, the Brave Bull is an extremely interesting combination of tequila (preferably blanco) and coffee liqueur. Build drink in a chilled old fashioned glass and stir gently. Serve on the rocks.

CANTARITO

50ml tequila
2 tsps fresh orange juice
2 tsps freshly squeezed lemon juice
2 tsps freshly squeezed lime juice
grapefruit soda
ice cubes
table salt
1 lime slice (optional)
1 lime twist (optional)
1 maraschino cherry (optional)

A not-so-distant cousin of the incredibly popular Paloma cocktail, the Cantarito takes the already successful combination of tequila, lime and grapefruit juice and throws in some orange, lemon and lime juice for good measure. Before you begin, rim a traditional Collins glass with salt, then fill with ice, tequila and fruit juices. Top up with grapefruit soda and garnish with lime and maraschino cherry.

CHIMAYO

50ml tequila
25ml unfiltered apple cider
2 tsps freshly squeezed lemon juice
1 tsp crème de cassis
ice cubes
2 apple slices (optional)

A New Mexican take on the classic apple and blackcurrant combination, the Chimayo is a delightful autumn crowd pleaser that is super simple to prepare. We recommend making your own unfiltered apple cider for the freshest taste; simply wash, core then puree some apples in a food processor, then press through a cheesecloth to extract the juice. Fill a traditional Old Fashioned glass with ice and stir well. Garnish with apple slices and serve. Legend has it that this cocktail was invented in the 1960s by Arturo Jaramillo to make use of his abundance of apples.

COCONUT TEQUILA

50 ml tequila
10 ml lemon juice
10 ml coconut cream
1 tsp maraschino liqueur

Place the ingredients in a blender with crushed ice and blitz for 15 seconds. Strain into an iced cocktail glass.

COLORADO SKIES

25 ml tequila
25 ml tequila
150 ml grapefruit juice

Place 2 or 3 ice cubes into a highball glass. Pour in the ingredients and stir. Optionally garnish with a slice of lime.

COMPADRE

50 ml tequila
10 ml Grenadine
5 ml maraschino liqueur
2 dashes orange bitters

Enhance your tequila with the help of bitter orange by pouring all of the ingredients above into an iced shaker before straining into a chilled cocktail glass.

ELDORADO

75 ml tequila
50 ml lemon juice
1 tbsp liquid honey

Try honey as a tasty way of softening the edges of the classic tequila and citrus combo. Shake all of the ingredients in an iced shaker. Place 3 ice cubes in a collins glass and strain your mixture into it. Optionally garnish with a slice of orange.

ENVY

50ml tequila
2 tsps blue curacao
1 tsp pineapple juice
crushed ice
1 pineapple wedge (optional)
1 maraschino cherry (optional)

Shake first four ingredients well in your Savisto Boston Cocktail Shaker, strain into a chilled cocktail glass over fresh ice and garnish with pineapple and cherries.

EXORCIST

50 ml tequila
25 ml blue curacao
25 ml lime juice

Fortunately, this is nowhere near as frightening as its name suggests. Pour the ingredients into an iced shaker. Shake well and strain into a cocktail glass.

FROZEN MARGARITA

75ml sour mix
50ml tequila
2 tsps freshly squeezed lime juice
2 tsps triple sec
ice cubes
table salt
1 slice of lime (optional)

This cold-as-ice reimagining of the classic Margarita takes everything you know and blends it up into a wonderful slush. We recommend trying your hand at using homemade sour mix for this recipe, but store bought will perform admirably either way. Pour all wet ingredients into a blender along with a handful of ice cubes and blitz until smooth. Add more ice cubes and keep pulsing until you find your desired consistency – you want this cocktail to look like a slushy. Chill a margarita glass, salt the rim and pour in the blended mixture. Garnish with a slice of lime and serve immediately under the summer sun.

GEORGIAN SUNRISE

25 ml tequila
15 ml peach schnapps
10 ml strawberry liqueur
100 ml sweet and sour mix

Combine all the ingredients in a collins glass and stir well. Add a couple of ice cubes and serve with a lime garnish.

GOLDEN RASPBERRY

25 ml tequila
25 ml Jägermeister
10 ml vodka
10 ml raspberry juice
10 ml Grenadine

!t hasn't taken long for everyone's favourite German hunting liqueur to start making an appearance in cocktails – and this one is based on a recipe straight from the Jägermeister stable. Pour all the ingredients in an iced shaker and shake well. Strain into a chilled cocktail glass.

HAWAIIAN ICED TEA

25ml fresh pineapple juice
25ml freshly squeezed lemon juice
2 tsps gin
2 tsps light rum
2 tsps tequila
2 tsps triple sec
2 tsps vodka
ice cubes
1 slice of lemon (optional)

Slowly build the ingredients in a collins glass, stir well and garnish with slice of lemon.

HAWAIIAN MARGARITA

50ml tequila
50g fresh pineapple
50g frozen strawberries
2 tsps triple sec
1 dash of sour mix
ice cubes
1 slice of jalapeno (optional)

This tropical take on the Margarita is bursting at the seams with fruity flavours and its icy consistency makes it the perfect compliment for the warm weather. Combine the tequila, pineapple, strawberries, triple sec and sour mix in a blender, add ice cubes and blitz until smooth. Add more ice if a thicker consistency is desired, or another dash or two of sour mix for a thinner drink. Chill a margarita glass, pour in mixture and garnish with a slice of jalapeno for a cool, fruity and warming summer beverage.

HORNY BULL

50ml tequila
orange juice
ice cubes
1 maraschino cherry (optional)
1 wedge of fresh lemon (optional)

Pour the shot of tequila over ice in a highball glass, top with orange juice and garnish.

HOT PANTS

50 ml tequila
15 ml peppermint schnapps
1 tbsp grapefruit juice
1 tsp powdered sugar

There's just the right proportion of peppermint in this one to complement rather than disguise the tequila... Shake up all the ingredients in an iced shaker and strain into a lowball glass rimmed with salt. Add a slice of lime to garnish.

JALAPENO MARGARITA

50ml tequila
25ml freshly squeezed lime juice
1 fresh jalapeño (plus extra for garnish)
2 tsps Grand Marnier
a dash of orange bitters
a dash of agave nectar
ice cubes

Deseed and slice the chili pepper and muddle in your Savisto Boston Cocktail Shaker. Shake well with the tequila, lime juice, Grand Marnier, orange bitters and agave nectar and strain over ice into a traditional highball glass. Garnish with additional jalapeno before serving.

JAMAICAN COOLER

25 ml tequila
25 ml blue curacao
25 ml coconut rum
10 ml pineapple juice

To be transported instantly to the Caribbean, mix together all of the listed ingredients in an iced shaker. Strain into a lowball glass with a couple of ice cubes at the bottom.

JIM'S DIABLO

50ml tequila
25ml freshly squeezed lemon juice
25ml ginger beer
1 tsp crème de cassis
ice cubes
1 wedge of lemon (optional)

Stir ingredients together over ice, strain into a chilled cocktail slice and serve with lemon wedge.

JUAN COLLINS

50ml tequila
25ml agave nectar
25ml freshly squeezed lemon juice
club soda
ice cubes
1 lime wedge (optional)

A distant Mexican ancestor of the Collins family, the Juan Collins is a quick, easy and refreshing drink that you'll savour all summer long. Fill a collins glass with ice cubes along with the tequila, agave nectar and lemon juice and stir well using your Savisto Twisted Bar Spoon. Top up with club soda, garnish with lemon wedge and serve.

LONG ISLAND ICED TEA

25ml sour mix
2 tsps gin
2 tsps rum
2 tsps tequila
2 tsps triple sec
2 tsps vodka
cola
ice cubes
1 lime wedge (optional)

A New York classic, the Long Island Iced Tea is a potent celebration of spirits that emerged in the 1970s and hasn't looked back since. Fill a Collins glass with ice and add the spirits and sour mix. Top up with cola, stir well and garnish with lime before serving. Beware, this household name may taste great but it certainly packs a punch, so drink in moderation.

MALIBU WAVE

25 ml tequila
10 ml triple sec
Dash blue curacao
50 ml sweet and sour mix

Despite its name, there's no Malibu rum in sight with this one… Shake all the ingredients with ice in a shaker and strain into a chilled cocktail glass. Garnish with a slice of lime and serve.

MARGARITA

50ml tequila
25ml freshly squeezed lime juice
2 tsps triple sec
ice cubes
1 lime slice (optional)
table salt (optional)

With a worldwide reputation, the Margarita carries a heavy burden as the household name of the tequila cocktail family. With such recognition comes dozens of variations - everyone loves a Margarita and everyone has their own idea of what makes the best - and we're no different. Before you begin, salt the rim of a chilled cocktail glass, then combine all the wet ingredients with ice in your Savisto Boston Cocktail Shaker and shake well. Pour the lot into the prepared glass (we think a neat Margarita is the most exquisite, but your mileage may vary) and garnish with lemon slice before serving.

MONTEZUMA

50 ml tequila
25 ml Madeira
1 egg yolk

The reasons why this creation is named after the famed Aztec emperor are lost in time. What's important is that it offers a tangy yet creamy way of enjoying your pre-dinner tequila. Place all the ingredients in a blender with half a cup of crushed ice. Blend at a low speed for 30 seconds before pouring into a champagne flute or cocktail glass.

PALOMA

50ml tequila
2 tsps freshly squeezed lime juice
grapefruit soda
ice cubes
1 lime slice (optional)
1 lime twist (optional)
1 maraschino cherry (optional)

Pour the tequila and lime juice in a collins glass over ice and top up with the grapefruit soda. Garnish with lime and cherry and serve.

PASSION COCKTAIL

50ml Grand Marnier
50ml tequila
25ml freshly squeezed lime juice
cranberry juice
ice cubes
1 lime twist (optional)

Shake the Grand Marnier, tequila and lime juice well with ice, strain into a chilled cocktail glass and top up with cranberry juice. Garnish with lime twist and serve.

STRAWBERRY MARGARITA

50ml tequila
25ml freshly squeezed lime juice
25ml triple sec
200g fresh strawberries
caster sugar (for rimming)
ice cubes
a few mint leaves (optional)

This decadent drink is arguably the most popular of all the flavoured Margaritas. Usually we'd recommend frozen fruit for this kind of recipe, but we find this combination of fresh strawberries and blended ice works even better. Add all ingredients (except sugar) to a blender, holding back a strawberry or two for garnish later, and blend until smooth. You can play around with the consistency here until you find something that matches your personal tastes, but you don't want this to be too thick to easily sip on a hot summer's day. Rim a chilled margarita glass with caster sugar, and pour the mixture into the glass. Garnish with strawberries and mint leaves to serve.

TEQUILA SUNRISE

50ml tequila
2 tsps of grenadine
fresh orange juice
ice cubes
1 orange twist (optional)
1 maraschino cherry (optional)

If you want to impress your guests with a majestic cocktail that doesn't take all that much effort, a Tequila Sunrise is right up your alley. From that first cut of sweetness right to the bottom of the glass, where the tequila settles and takes prominence, every second of this wonderful beverage is a joy to behold. Fill a traditional Highball glass with ice then pour in the tequila and top up with orange juice, stopping just shy of the brim. Stir well then slowly pour in the grenadine around the side of the glass. This will create the desired sunrise effect naturally - it really is as simple as that. Garnish with orange twist and maraschino cherry and serve with a straw.

TEQUINI

75ml tequila
2 tsps dry vermouth
a dash of Angostura bitters
red chili and jalapeño slices (optional)

In your Savisto Boston Cocktail Shaker, shake together the tequila, dry vermouth and bitters well. Strain into a chilled cocktail glass using your Savisto Hawthorne Strainer and garnish with slices of chili on a cocktail stick for a fiery kick.

TORONHA

50ml tequila
25ml fresh grapefruit juice
25ml fresh watermelon juice
25ml freshly squeezed lemon juice
2 tsps grenadine
2 tsps triple sec
ice cubes
1 wedge of fresh lemon (optional)
1 wedge of fresh watermelon (optional)
skewered grapes (optional)

Blend ingredients well with ice until smooth, pour into a chilled sour glass and garnish with fruit.

Arguably the most popular spirit on the market, thanks to its mostly neutral flavour, aroma and colour making it ideal for combining with limitless assortments of other flavours. In the cocktail world, vodka often sits in the background, allowing the other natural flavours to shine, but offering a depth unlike anything else.

On top of that, vodka now comes in almost any flavour you could imagine. Fruit and herb infused spirits are widely available, and you can even find a tobacco flavoured vodka if you look hard enough, though we wouldn't recommend using that in your White Russian.

It's important to remember that, with vodka, you get what you pay for. If you skimp on the quality of your spirits, your cocktails will suffer as a result, so please, always go for the purer top shelf options. Your tastebuds (and your stomach lining) will thank you for it.

ALABAMA SLAMMER

2 tsps Amaretto
2 tsps sloe gin
2 tsps Southern Comfort
2 tsps vodka
orange juice
ice cubes
1 slice of lemon (optional)

This is a twist on the classic party drink of the 80s, throwing vodka into the already explosive mix of Amaretto and Southern Comfort. Don't worry, though, even the strongest of vodkas won't overpower this cocktail, it simply adds a tantalizing depth of flavour. Fill a traditional Highball glass with ice, add all four alcoholic elements and top up with orange juice. Stir well, garnish with lemon slice and serve.

APPLETINI

50ml vodka
25ml apple schnapps
1 maraschino cherry (optional)

An Apple Martini (or Appletini) will vary depending on where you order from, but the two most important elements remain universally the same. The sour combination of vodka and apple (be it from fresh apple juice, calvados or an apple liqueur) is still an incredibly popular choice worldwide, but we prefer the sweeter option of apple schnapps. Pour the vodka and schnapps into your Savisto Boston Cocktail Shaker along with a handful of ice and shake well. Strain into a chilled cocktail glass using your Savisto Hawthorne Strainer and garnish with a maraschino cherry.

AUBURN

75ml orange juice
50ml vodka
50ml Galliano
25ml crème de cassis
ice cubes

Pour all the ingredients into a cocktail shaker filled with ice and shake well, Strain into a cocktail glass to serve. Add an orange twist as a garnish (optional).

BALALAIKA

50ml freshly squeezed lemon juice
50ml vodka
25ml Cointreau
ice cubes

Add all the ingredients into an iced cocktail shaker. After shaking up, strain into a cocktail glass.

BAY BREEZE

50ml vodka
cranberry juice
pineapple juice
ice cubes
1 wedge of lime (optional)
1 maraschino cherry (optional)

Another classic combination of vodka and fruit juices, the Bay Breeze isn't far removed from the Cape Codder (found later in this chapter), but adds the tang of pineapple to the already fantastic vodka and cranberry combo. This effortless and elegant mixed drink is the perfect refreshment for sharing out at picnics and barbeques in the summer. Fill a traditional Highball glass with ice and pour in the vodka. Top up with equal parts cranberry and pineapple juices, then dip in the maraschino cherry and garnish with lime wedge.

BLACK MAGIC
50ml black vodka
2 tsps grenadine
lemon & lime soda
ice cubes
1 maraschino cherry (optional)

Build the ingredients over ice in a traditional collins glass, top up with soda and garnish with cherry.

BLACK RUSSIAN
50ml vodka
25ml coffee liqueur
ice cubes

Even since its invention in 1949, the Black Russian still stands mightily at the top of every cocktail connoisseur's wishlist. There's just something about the simple hit of coffee bursting through the vodka that endures all other passing trends. Combine the ingredients in a traditional Old Fashioned glass, stir well and serve on the rocks. No frills, just thrills.

BLOODY CAESAR

50ml vodka
2 dashes of Worcestershire sauce
1 dash of tabasco sauce
celery salt
clamato juice
freshly ground black pepper
1 celery stalk (optional)
1 lemon wedge (optional)

A Canadian take on the Bloody Mary, some might argue that the Caesar (simply switching tomato juice out for clamato juice) even blows the more popular Mary away. The addition of clam may be somewhat of an acquired taste, but if you can get past that, you'll be in business. Rim a Highball glass with lemon juice and celery salt to start with, then fill with ice cubes and add the vodka shots. Top up with clamato juice, then season with Worcestershire sauce, tabasco sauce and black pepper. Using your Savisto Twisted Bar Spoon, stir well to combine all the flavours and garnish with celery stalk and lemon wedge for an unparalleled answer to your hangover woes.

BLOODY MARY

75ml tomato juice
50ml vodka
2 tsps freshly squeezed lemon juice
a dash of horseradish sauce
a dash of tabasco sauce
a dash of Worcestershire sauce
a pinch of celery salt
a pinch of freshly ground black pepper
ice cubes
1 celery stalk (optional)

The ultimate hangover cure. Build the ingredients over ice in a chilled highball glass and stir well. Garnish with celery stalk.

BLUE BIRD

75ml vodka
25ml Cointreau
25ml lemon juice
3 dashes maraschino
3 dashes blue colouring extract
ice cubes

The blue extract in this drink isn't an absolute requirement, but is highly recommended for that crowd-pleasing electric blue effect. Shake all ingredients with ice in a cocktail shaker before straining into a chilled cocktail glass.

BLUEBERRY MARTINI

50ml blueberry juice
50ml vodka
25ml mango juice
2 tsps orange liqueur
ice cubes
½ a fresh strawberry (optional)

In your Savisto Boston Cocktail Shaker, shake the vodka, fruit juices, liqueur and ice cubes well. Strain into a chilled cocktail glass and drop in the strawberry for garnish.

BOCCE BALL

50ml vodka
2 tsps amaretto
a splash of soda water
orange juice
ice cubes
1 wedge of fresh orange (optional)

Fill a Collins glass with ice and build the drink slowly, finishing by topping up the glass with orange juice. Garnish with orange segment and serve.

BULL SHOT

75ml beef bouillon
50ml vodka
2 dashes of tabasco sauce
2 dashes of Worcestershire sauce
a dash of freshly squeezed lemon juice
a pinch of celery salt
freshly ground black pepper
ice cubes
1 lemon wedge (optional)

Cut the bull with this unusual (but delightful) drink, typically served warm in the winter months. While the ingredients list may read more like a soup or broth recipe, you'll find plenty of cocktail menus proudly boasting this. Fill your Savisto Cocktail Shaker with ice and shake together the vodka, bouillon, tabasco, Worcestershire, lemon juice, celery salt and pepper. Fill a Highball glass with ice and strain the mixture in with your Savisto Hawthorne Strainer. Drop in a wedge of lemon and serve.

CAMPARI

75ml Campari
50ml vodka
a dash of Angostura bitters
ice cubes
1 lemon twist (optional)

Pour all ingredients into a cocktail shaker filled with ice cubes. Shake well before straining into a chilled cocktail glass. Garnish with a lemon twist to serve.

CAPE CODDER

75ml cranberry juice
50ml vodka
ice cubes
1 lime wedge (optional)

An incredibly popular Highball drink that keeps things short and sweet, the Cape Codder is one of those fantastic and simple cocktails that combines a spirit with fruit juice and lets the flavours do the talking. Those flavours, in this instance, are the winning combination of vodka and cranberry; a tried and tested fusion that's stood the test of time. Throw them together into a traditional Highball glass filled with ice and stir well. Squeeze a touch of lime juice in there, then garnish with the wedge.

CARROT CAKE

50ml vodka
25ml carrot juice
2 tsps whole milk
2 tsps allspice (plus extra for garnish)
a splash of soda water
ice cubes

Shake all ingredients bar soda water over ice, strain into a cocktail glass and top up with soda. Garnish with a final pinch of allspice.

CATAMARAN

75ml fresh pineapple juice
50ml freshly squeezed lemon juice
50ml rum
50ml vodka
1 tsp caster sugar
a dash of grenadine

Build all the ingredients in a tall glass, finishing with the dash of grenadine. Add a twist of lemon as an optional garnish.

CHERRY VODKA

50ml freshly squeezed lime juice
50ml vodka
25ml cherry brandy
ice cubes
1 maraschino cherry (optional)

Add all the ingredients to an ice-filled cocktail shaker. After shaking well, strain into a cocktail glass and add the cherry to garnish.

CHOCOLATE MARTINI

50ml vodka
50ml creme de cacao
cocoa powder
freshly squeezed orange juice
ice cubes
1 orange twist (optional)

The Chocolate Martini is a cocktail that begs you to explore different flavour combinations. Chocolate is such a versatile ingredient that is complimented well by all manner of flavours - orange, vanilla or blackcurrant, to name just a few - and there's really no right or wrong answer here. You can experiment with infused vodkas if you wish, but we find a straight, premium vodka is simple but effective. Fill your Savisto Boston Cocktail Shaker with ice cubes and shake the vodka and creme de cacao together to combine well. In the meantime, rim a chilled cocktail glass with the cocoa powder and a touch of orange juice, then strain in the contents of the shaker using your Savisto Hawthorne Strainer. Finish with a final hit of juice, then garnish with the orange twist.

COCONUT MARTINI

50ml vodka
25ml coconut rum
2 tsps coconut cream
a splash of pineapple juice
desiccated coconut (optional)

For fans of the Pina Colada, the Coconut Martini is a classic, tropical vodka martini that really hits the spot. Shake the vodka, rum and coconut cream well to combine in your Savisto Boston Cocktail Shaker, strain into a chilled cocktail glass and top with a pinch of desiccated coconut.

COLORADO BULLDOG

25ml vodka
25ml coffee liqueur
double cream
cola
ice cubes

Taking inspiration from the White Russian, the Colorado Bulldog differs by adding a cola element, which makes for a refreshing change of pace if you're a little tired of the standard fare. Fill a traditional Old Fashioned glass with ice cubes, then pour in the vodka and coffee liqueur. Top up the glass with equal parts cola and double cream, stir well and serve.

COSMOPOLITAN

75ml vodka
50ml Cointreau
25ml freshly squeezed lime juice
2 tsps fresh cranberry juice
ice cubes
1 orange peel (optional)

Fill a cocktail shaker with ice and pour in all the ingredients. Shake well before straining into a chilled cocktail glass. Garnish with the orange peel.

ESPRESSO MARTINI

50ml vodka
25ml espresso
25ml kahlua
1 tsp crème de cacao
ice cubes
1 coffee bean (optional)

Once your espresso has cooled, shake it well with the vodka, kahlua, crème de cacao and ice cubes. Strain into a chilled cocktail glass and garnish with a coffee bean.

FIREFLY

50ml vodka
25ml grenadine
grapefruit juice
ice cubes
1 lemon slice (optional)

This sweet and tart cocktail takes the winning formula of the Greyhound (vodka and grapefruit juice) and throws in a shot of grenadine for balance. This simple addition transforms the entire drink into something entirely different, and even gives it a Tequila Sunrise inspired gradient effect. Fill a traditional Highball glass with ice, pour in the vodka and top up with grapefruit juice. Finally, add the shot of grenadine and marble with your Savisto Twisted Bar Spoon. Garnish with lemon slice and serve.

FLIRTINI

25ml pineapple juice
2 fresh pineapple chunks
2 tsps Cointreau
2 tsps vodka
champagne
1 maraschino cherry (optional)
1 orange slice (optional)

Like the Cosmopolitan before it, the Flirtini is the perfect drink for special occasions, only this one swaps out cranberry and lime for champagne and pineapple juice. Using your Savisto Wooden Muddler, muddle the pineapple chunks and Cointreau in the bottom of your Savisto Boston Mixing Glass. Add the vodka and a shot of pineapple juice, stir well, then strain into a chilled cocktail glass using your Savisto Hawthorne Strainer. Top up the glass with champagne, then finish with orange garnish and a maraschino cherry. Serve immediately before the champagne loses its fizz.

GODMOTHER
50ml vodka
2 tsps Amaretto
ice cubes
1 orange twist (optional)

The softer spouse of the Hollywood-inspired Godfather, the Godmother is an extremely simple combination of vodka and the almond-flavoured liqueur Amaretto that will leave your tastebuds tingling. As its name suggests, the Godmother has a reputation for being the more feminine choice for an on the rocks lowball, but this mixed drink is just too good to subscribe to such gender roles. Stir the vodka and Amaretto together in a traditional Old Fashioned glass and serve on the rocks with an orange twist for garnish.

GOLDFINGER
75ml vodka
50ml pineapple juice
25ml Galliano
ice cubes

Combine all the ingredients in a cocktail shaker filled with ice. Shake well and strain into a chilled cocktail glass.

GRAND DUCHESS

75ml vodka
50ml freshly squeezed lime juice
50ml rum
25ml Grenadine
ice cubes

Pour all the ingredients into an ice-filled cocktail shaker before shaking well. Strain into a chilled cocktail glass.

GREYHOUND

50ml vodka
grapefruit juice
ice cubes
1 lemon slice (optional)

The beauty of the Greyhound lies in the background noise. Vodka will never overpower the sharp taste of grapefruit; instead hiding behind it to provide a subtle accent depending on the vodka you use. Feel free to experiment with different infusions - especially berry vodkas - as this will bring another layer of flavour with it. Fill a collins glass with ice cubes, add the vodka, and top up with grapefruit juice. Stir well, garnish with lemon slice and serve.

HAIRY NAVEL

25ml vodka
25ml peach schnapps
orange juice
ice cubes
1 orange slice (optional)

A relative of the Fuzzy Navel, this fruity drink simply has more hair on its chest. The addition of vodka doesn't overwhelm, but adds an element of spice to this otherwise sweet cocktail. Fill a traditional Highball glass with ice cubes and combine with the vodka and peach schnapps. Top up with orange juice, stir well and garnish with orange slice.

HARVEY WALLBANGER
50ml orange juice
25ml vodka
1 tsp Galliano
ice cubes
1 lime wedge (optional)

A survivor of the 70s disco scene, the Harvey Wallbanger has taken on a cultural significance beyond just the world of cocktails. Stop anybody in the street and they're likely to have at least heard of this makeshift mixed drink. Fill a traditional collins glass with ice cubes along with the orange juice, vodka and Galliano. Allow to settle before garnishing with a wedge of lime and serve. Champion.

HEARTBEAT
50ml light rum
50ml vodka
50ml passion fruit liqueur
a splash of fresh orange juice
a splash of fresh pineapple juice
ice cubes

Mix the all the ingredients in a cocktail shaker with ice and shake well. Strain into a cocktail glass and add a twist of orange as an optional garnish.

HOLIDAY MARTINI

25ml vodka
25ml fresh orange juice
25ml peach schnapps
25ml pomegranate juice
a dash of freshly squeezed lemon juice
ice cubes
1 orange twist (optional)

Mix ingredients well with ice in your Savisto Boston Cocktail Shaker. Strain into a chilled cocktail glass, garnish with orange twist and serve.

HOLLYWOOD MARTINI

75ml vodka
2 tsps raspberry liqueur
pineapple juice
1 orange twist (optional)

The Hollywood Martini is almost a carbon copy of the Raspberry Smash, the only difference being that it's shaken (not stirred) and served neat. It makes for an ideal summer refreshment, as with most fruit-flavoured cocktails. Fill your Savisto Boston Cocktail Shaker with ice, pour in vodka and raspberry liqueur and shake well. Strain into a chilled cocktail glass using your Savisto Hawthorne Strainer, top up with pineapple juice, garnish with orange twist and serve.

IGUANA

25 ml vodka
25 ml tequila
10 ml coffee liqueur
50 ml sweet and sour mix

For a mellow and aromatic take on tequila, take all of the ingredients listed above and pour them into an iced shaker. Shake well and strain into a chilled cocktail glass. Garnish with a slice of lime.

IRISH MARTINI

50ml vodka
2 tsps dry vermouth
2 tsps whiskey
cracked ice
1 lemon twist (optional)

What makes this Martini Irish? It's a hit of whiskey, and even this small amount will transform what you think you know about the Martini, adding a depth, flavour and texture you never could have imagined. Don't think about skimping on quality here; cocktails such as this rely on the premium flavours of its bare ingredients. In a chilled cocktail glass, add the whiskey and swirl around until well coated and discard the excess. Half fill your Savisto Boston Cocktail Shaker with cracked ice and add the vodka and vermouth. Shake well, strain into the coated glass using your Savisto Hawthorne Strainer and garnish with lemon twist before serving. It might seem like a lot of effort for such a small amount, but trust us on this one; you won't be wasting a single second.

JAEGER

50ml vodka
50ml dry sherry
25ml Grand Marnier
Dash orange bitters
ice cubes

Nothing to do with Jägermeister, this cocktail dates back to the 1920s and was an invention of Café Royal bartender, Charles J. Jaeger. Stir the ingredients together in a mixing glass with ice. Pour into a cocktail glass and serve with a cherry and lemon peel for a garnish.

KAMIKAZE

50ml vodka
25ml freshly squeezed lime juice
25ml triple sec
ice cubes
1 lime twist (optional)

Lying somewhere between a Daiquiri and a Margarita, the Kamikaze sure packs a punch, as the name might suggest. On its own, this is quite a naked cocktail, but with a wide choice of infused vodkas available, you have room to experiment with whatever works for you. Pour the vodka, lime juice and triple sec into your Savisto Boston Cocktail Shaker along with ice cubes and shake well to combine. Strain into a chilled cocktail glass using your Savisto Hawthorne Strainer and garnish with the lime twist before serving.

KEY LIME PIE MARTINI

50ml vodka
25ml pineapple juice
2 tsps freshly squeezed lime juice
2 tsps triple sec
ice cubes
demerara sugar (optional)
1 slice of fresh lime (optional)

Shake vodka, fruit juices and triple sec well with ice in your Savisto Boston Cocktail Shaker and strain into a chilled cocktail glass rimmed with demerara sugar. Garnish with lime and serve.

KIWI MARTINI

75ml vodka
1 tsp caster sugar
½ a kiwifruit
ice cubes
1 kiwi fruit slice (optional)

If you're a fan of the sweet and sour green flesh of the kiwifruit, this is the perfect Martini for you. You'll find different variations of this cocktail kicking around, but ours uses sugar to balance the tartness of the fruit, leaving you with a completely sweet and indulgent drink. In your Savisto Boston Cocktail Shaker, muddle together the kiwifruit flesh and sugar using your Savisto Wooden Muddler. Add vodka and a handful of ice cubes and shake well. Strain into a chilled cocktail glass using your Savisto Hawthorne Strainer, garnish with kiwifruit slice and serve.

LAVENDER DROP

50ml vodka
25ml freshly squeezed lemon juice
2 tsps caster sugar
a sprig of fresh lavender (plus extra for garnish)
ice cubes

A take on the original Lemon Drop, this version incorporates the fresh burst of lavender to take this cocktail to the next level. Muddle the sprig of lavender with the sugar in the bottom of your Savisto Boston Cocktail Shaker in order to release the natural aroma and oils of the flower. Add the vodka, lemon juice and ice cubes and shake well. Strain into a chilled cocktail glass and garnish with additional lavender.

LEMON DROP MARTINI

50ml vodka
25ml freshly squeezed lemon juice
1 tsp caster sugar (plus extra for rimming)
ice cubes
1 lemon twist (optional)

If what you look for in a cocktail is the same as you look for in candy, this sweet and sour dessert Martini will blow you away. The beauty of this cocktail is that it is open to interpretation; you can alter the balance by changing the quantities of sugar and lemon juice, or even experiment with flavoured vodkas. We prefer this on the bitter side, almost approaching something like sherbet. Before you begin, rim the edges of a chilled cocktail glass with sugar and lemon juice. Pour the vodka, lemon juice and caster sugar into your Savisto Boston Cocktail Shaker along with a generous handful of ice cubes. Shake well and strain into the prepared glass using your Savisto Hawthorne Strainer. Garnish with lemon twist and serve.

MADRAS
75ml cranberry juice
50ml vodka
orange juice
ice cubes
1 lime twist (optional)

The Madras cocktail is super simple to remember, making it perfect for your repertoire of drinks to knock out with minimal effort. Despite its name, the Madras isn't an Indian inspired drink; rather, it's more reminiscent of the Cosmopolitan, albeit a touch mellower than its Sex in the City cousin. Pour the cranberry juice and vodka into a traditional Highball glass, along with a handful of ice cubes. Stir well, top up with orange juice and garnish with lime twist.

MARY ROSE
50ml vodka
2 tsps cranberry juice
2 tsps crème de cassis
1 sprig of fresh rosemary
club soda
ice cubes
1 maraschino cherry (optional)

Shake the ice cubes, vodka, cranberry juice, crème de cassis and rosemary well to infuse the herb with the rest of the ingredients. Strain into a chilled cocktail glass, top up with club soda and garnish with maraschino cherry.

MELONTINI

25ml vodka
25ml melon juice
2 tsps caster sugar
a few slices of cucumber (plus extra for garnish)
ice cubes

Muddle the cucumber and sugar in the bottom of your Savisto Boston Cocktail Shaker to release the cucumber's aroma. Add the vodka and melon juice and shake well to combine. Strain into a chilled cocktail glass, garnish with an additional slice of cucumber and serve.

MOSCOW MULE

50ml vodka
25ml freshly squeezed lime juice
ginger beer
ice cubes
1 lime slice (optional)
1 maraschino cherry (optional)

Legend has it that the Moscow Mule originates in Hollywood, where John Martin - head of Smirnoff at the time - sought to promote vodka to the new market in the United States. The rest, as they say, is history, and this fun cocktail has remained a popular choice ever since, though recipes vary. The most crucial aspect of the Moscow Mule is the use of a ginger beer, not ale, as the primary ingredient. As recently as 2014, the Mule saw a huge resurgence, and it's easy to see why once you've sampled this drink. Fill a traditional Highball glass (or copper mug, if you're feeling authentic) with ice cubes and pour in the vodka and lime juice. Stir well to combine, then top up the glass with ginger beer. Garnish with the slice of lime and maraschino cherry and serve.

MUDSLIDE
25ml coffee liqueur
25ml Irish cream liqueur
25ml vodka
chocolate syrup
ice cubes
ground cinnamon (optional)

A spinoff of the White Russian, this fantastically indulgent drink takes the popular vodka cocktail and replaces cream with Irish cream liqueur and lashings of chocolate sauce. Pour the vodka and liqueurs into your Savisto Boston Cocktail Shaker along with a generous handful of ice cubes. Shake well, fill a traditional Old Fashioned glass with ice, and strain the mixture in using your Savisto Hawthorne Strainer. Drizzle with a cascade of chocolate sauce to drizzle down the sides and top with a dusting of ground cinnamon.

NUTTY MARTINI
50ml vodka
25ml hazelnut liqueur
2 tsps caster sugar
1 fresh raspberry (optional)
ground pecans (optional)

Half fill your Savisto Boston Cocktail Shaker with ice and pour in the vodka, caster sugar and hazelnut liqueur. Shake well, then strain into a cocktail glass using your Savisto Hawthorne Strainer. Garnish with ground pecans and a single raspberry on a cocktail stick. This is a wonderfully dark and nutty Martini that'll leave your tastebuds tingling.

NUTTY VODKA & COKE

75ml vodka
25ml amaretto
cola
ice cubes

Add the vodka and amaretto to a cocktail shaker filled with ice. Shake well, then strain into a highball glass. Half fill with ice cubes before topping up with Coke.

OLD COUNTRY MARTINI

100 ml vodka
25 ml Madeira
25 ml cherry brandy

For this intensely rich and dark variation of the martini, pour all the ingredients into a mixing glass with a good handful of cracked ice. Stir well before straining into a chilled cocktail glass. Add an orange twist to garnish.

ORANGE VODKA MARTINI

75ml vodka
50ml dry vermouth
50ml triple sec
a dash of orange bitters
cracked ice
1 orange twist (optional)

Half-fill a cocktail shaker with cracked ice before pouring in all the ingredients. Shake well and then strain into a cocktail glass. Garnish with the orange twist to serve.

PALM BEACH
75ml vodka
50ml fresh grapefruit juice
25ml crème de cassis
25ml freshly squeezed lemon juice
2 tsps caster sugar
ice cubes

Combine all ingredients in a cocktail shaker with ice. Shake well and strain into a chilled cocktail glass. To serve, garnish with a twist of orange.

PEARL HARBOUR
75ml vodka
50ml melon liqueur
fresh pineapple juice
ice cubes
1 maraschino cherry (optional)
fresh pineapple wedges (optional)

In a lowball glass filled with ice, add the vodka and melon liqueur. Fill with pineapple juice and garnish with the skewered cherry and pineapple chunks.

PUMPKIN MARTINI

75ml vanilla vodka
50ml cream liqueur
50ml pumpkin liqueur
1 tsp whipped cream
ice cubes
1 cinnamon stick (optional)

Add the cream liqueur and vodka into an ice-filled cocktail shaker and shake well. Add the pumpkin liqueur and give it another shake. Strain into a chilled cocktail glass, top with whipped cream and garnish with the cinnamon stick.

SCREWDRIVER

50ml vodka
orange juice
ice cubes
1 lime wedge (optional)

Arguably the drink that started the trend when it came to popular vodka cocktails, the Screwdriver is a classic combination of vodka and orange juice that has remained a favourite for many for decades. Fill a traditional Collins glass with ice cubes, pour in the vodka and orange and stir well. Garnish with the lime wedge and serve.

SEA BREEZE

75ml cranberry juice
50ml vodka
25ml grapefruit juice
ice cubes
2 lime wedges (optional)

The Sea Breeze is another of those classic vodka and fruit juice cocktails and should be on every cocktail enthusiast's repertory. This stunning drink doesn't just look the part; it tastes great under any circumstances. Stir the vodka, cranberry and grapefruit juices together in a Highball glass - use your Savisto Twisted Bar Spoon - fill glass with ice and lime wedges and top up with more grapefruit juice to create a gorgeous gradient effect.

SEX ON THE BEACH

50ml cranberry juice
50ml orange juice
50ml vodka
25ml peach schnapps
2 tsps creme de cassis
ice cubes
3 mango wedges (optional)

It's entirely possible that this is the most recognised cocktail on the planet. It's an unparalleled tropical delight that's ideally enjoyed under a parasol, but just as good at your nearest cocktail lounge on a winter evening. Fill your Savisto Boston Cocktail Shaker with ice cubes, vodka, peach schnapps, creme de cassis and fruit juices and shake well. Fill a traditional Highball glass with ice cubes and strain the mixture in using your Savisto Hawthorne Strainer. Garnish with mango wedges and serve.

SHALOM

50 ml vodka
25 ml Madeira
2 dashes orange juice

The neutrality of vodka is often set off with orange in cocktails. Here, there's just a hint of orange side-by-side the richness of Madeira. To create it, shake all the ingredients with ice in a cocktail shaker. Throw a couple of ice cubes into a lowball glass and strain in the ingredients. Garnish with a slice of orange before serving.

SMITH & WESSON

75ml whole milk
50ml coffee liqueur
50ml vodka
club soda
ice cubes

Pour the vodka, liqueur and milk into an ice-filled highball glass. Fill with club soda before serving.

TERRAZZA

50ml vodka
50ml Galliano
75ml pineapple juice
25ml single cream
ice cubes

Combine all ingredients in an iced cocktail shaker and shake well. Strain into a chilled cocktail glass and garnish with a cherry.

UPSTARTER
50ml vodka
50ml Galliano
25ml peach brandy
ice cubes

Shake the ingredients in an iced cocktail shaker before straining into a chilled cocktail glass.

VERY BERRY
50ml blueberry vodka
2 tsps cranberry juice
2 tsps raspberry liquer
2 tsps triple sec
ice cubes

Fill your Savisto Boston Cocktail Shaker with ice and shake vodka, cranberry juice and liqueurs until well combined. Strain into a chilled cocktail glass and serve.

VODKA COLLINS
50ml vodka
25ml freshly squeezed lemon juice
2 tsps caster sugar
club soda
ice cubes
1 orange slice (optional)

The delightful Collins family combine spirits, sours and soda to create a delightfully refreshing drink for those days under the sun. Pour the vodka, lemon juice and sugar into a Collins glass over ice and stir well until sugar is dissolved. Top up glass with club soda and garnish with orange slice before serving on the rocks.

VODKA GRASSHOPPER
75ml vodka
50ml crème de menthe
50ml crème de cacao
ice cubes

Tracing its roots back to the New Orleans French Quarter, this is a sweet and minty treat that's perfect as an after dinner drink. Shake all the ingredients in an iced cocktail shaker before straining into a chilled cocktail glass.

VODKA MARTINI
50ml vodka
25ml dry vermouth
2 dashes of bitters
ice cubes
1 lemon twist (optional)

Shake ingredients well in your Savisto Boston Cocktail Shaker with ice, strain into a chilled cocktail glass and garnish with lemon twist.

VODKA OLD FASHIONED
75ml vodka
1/2 tsp sugar
2 dashes aromatic bitters
ice cubes

Build the ingredients in a lowball glass. Fill with ice and add a lemon twist or cherry as a garnish.

VODKA RED BULL
75ml vodka
red bull
ice cubes

Fill a highball glass with ice before adding the vodka. Fill with Red Bull and serve.

VODKA TONIC
50ml vodka
tonic water
freshly squeezed lime juice (to taste)
ice cubes
1 lime wedge (optional)

Although maybe not quite as popular as its gin cousin, the Vodka Tonic is cleaner and more refreshing thanks to the cut of lime and less overpowering base spirit. Please do not skimp on a cheap brand of vodka; all this will do is cheapen your final product. With drinks such as this that rely on just a couple of flavours, it's important to use premium ingredients as their deficiencies cannot be disguised. Fill a traditional Highball glass with ice and pour in the vodka and lime juice. Top up glass with tonic and stir well. Garnish with lime and serve.

VOLGA BOATMAN

75ml vodka
50ml cherry brandy
50ml orange juice
ice cubes

Combine the ingredients in an iced cocktail shaker and shake well before straining into a chilled cocktail glass.

WARSAW

75ml vodka
25ml blackberry liqueur
25ml dry vermouth
10ml fresh lemon juice
ice cubes

Shake all ingredients together in an iced cocktail shaker before straining into a chilled cocktail glass. Add a twist of lemon for garnish.

WHITE RUSSIAN

50ml vodka
25ml coffee liqueur
25ml double cream
ice cubes

A mixed drink that was forever immortalised by The Dude, the White

Russian only has a couple of simple steps to abide by. Build the ingredients in a traditional Old Fashioned glass over ice and stir until combined. There are dozens of derivatives of the White Russian, but few, if any, can eclipse this delightful combination of vodka and coffee liqueur.

WOO WOO
50ml cranberry juice
25ml peach schnapps
25ml vodka
ice cubes
1 maraschino cherry (optional)

One of the first cocktails to be learned by any aspiring bartender, the Woo Woo is a popular fruity Highball sipped across cocktail lounges all around the world. Combine all ingredients in your Savisto Boston Cocktail Shaker and shake well to combine the flavours. Strain into a chilled Highball glass using your Savisto Hawthorne Strainer and garnish with maraschino cherry before serving.

Arguably the most complicated of the distilled spirits, the intricate combinations of aged grains and spices in whiskey produce perhaps the most satisfying drinking experience. Whiskey drinkers tend to be inherently loyal to their drink of choice, so much so that it defines their entire characters. Iconic images in film show the refined gentlemen of yesteryear, sleeves rolled up casually as they pour their scotch on the rocks after a long day of presumably masculine graft.

There are so many varieties of whiskey that it can be overwhelming for new drinkers, but you can't go wrong with keeping a few choice selections at hand, namely Irish whisky, scotch, bourbon and rye whiskey. With this basic assortment, you can find the flavour for you before delving deeper into the rabbit hole.

Thanks to its usually high volume, whiskey carries a reputation for being a hard drink for harder men (and women), but this is most assuredly not the case. Whiskey has outlived the eighteenth century binge drinkers to form a distinct fan-base of passionate drinkers. Its artisanal properties almost make it somewhat hipster, but there's never been a stronger selection of whiskeys with which to treat yourself. If you haven't yet delved into this layer cake, now is the perfect time to jump on board.

7&7

50ml whiskey
lemon & lime soda
ice cubes
1 lemon wedge (optional)

The recipe calls for two specific ingredients (Seagram's 7 Crown Whiskey and 7-Up) from which it gets its name. Pour the shot of whiskey over ice in a traditional highball glass, top up with soda and garnish with lemon wedge.

AFFINITY

25ml scotch
2 dashes orange bitters
2 tsps dry vermouth
2 tsps sweet vermouth

Combined with the mellow tones of a single malt scotch, the Affinity makes for a great aperitif. Stir the scotch, bitters and vermouths well into a cocktail glass and serve neat.

ALE COCKTAIL

50ml whisky
ginger beer
juice of ½ a freshly squeezed lemon
ice cubes
1 wedge of fresh lemon (optional)

Squeeze the lemon over ice in a traditional highball glass. Add the whisky, fill with ginger beer and stir before garnish with lemon wedge.

ALGONQUIN COCKTAIL

50ml whiskey
25ml dry vermouth
25ml pineapple juice
ice cubes
1 lime twist (optional)

Shake ingredients well with ice, strain into a chilled cocktail glass and garnish with lime.

APPLE PIE

50ml cranberry juice
50ml whisky
25ml apple schnapps
ice cubes
1 apple wedge (optional)

Shake ingredients together with ice and strain into a chilled martini glass. Garnish with apple and serve.

AUTUMN WINDS

25ml whisky
25ml cinnamon schnapps
2 dashes of Angostura bitters
apple cider
ice cubes
1 cinnamon stick (optional)

As the sun sets on a summer's night for the final time, there's no better cocktail to usher in the autumn months. The Autumn Winds evokes feelings of crisp, vivid leaves beneath your feet and the cool accompanying breeze.

Combine the whisky, schnapps and bitters in a bucket glass over ice and top up with apple cider. Stir gently, garnish with cinnamon stick and serve.

AVENUE
50 ml bourbon
50 ml calcados
50 ml passion fruit juice
Dash grenadine
Dash orange flower water

The end result here should be light, refreshing and ever-so-slightly floral in tone. Simply shake up all the ingredients in an iced cocktail shaker and strain into a cocktail glass.

BELMONT JEWEL
50ml bourbon
50ml lemonade
25ml fresh pomegranate juice
ice cubes
1 wedge of lime (optional)
1 maraschino cherry (optional)

A fresh, delicious and wholly satisfying cocktail, the Belmont Jewel is the ideal summer refreshment. Shake ingredients well in your Savisto Boston Cocktail Shaker, strain into a highball glass, garnish and serve on the rocks.

BLACK & RED
25ml whisky
2 dashes of Angostura bitters
2 tsps sweet vermouth
ice cubes

The distant Irish cousin of the Manhattan, the Black & Red calls for the use of a sweeter whisky as opposed to rye. Stir the ingredients together in your Savisto Boston Mixing Glass and strain into a traditional Old Fashioned glass using your Savisto Hawthorne Strainer. Serve neat.

THE BLACK NAIL
25ml whisky
25ml honey liqueur
ice cubes
1 orange twist (optional)

Build ingredients in an old fashioned glass over ice. Garnish with orange peel and serve.

BLACKBERRY MALT
50ml whisky
25ml freshly squeezed lime juice
3 tsps caster sugar
crushed ice
fresh blackberries
sparkling water

Muddle a small handful of blackberries with the caster sugar and add to your Savisto Boston Cocktail Shaker with the whisky, lime juice and ice cubes. Strain into highball glass on the rocks, top up with sparkling water and drop in a few more fresh blackberries.

THE BLINKER

75 ml rye whiskey
50 ml grapefruit juice
25 ml grenadine

For this variation on a classic blend of rye and grapefruit, shake the ingredients with ice in a cocktail shaker and strain into a cocktail glass.

BLOOD & SAND

25ml cherry brandy
25ml fresh orange juice
25ml scotch
25ml sweet vermouth
ice cubes
1 orange twist (optional)

With equal parts brandy, orange juice, scotch and sweet vermouth, the Blood and Sand is a fantastic recipe to have in your arsenal. Shake the elements together with ice in your Savisto Boston Cocktail Shaker, strain into a cocktail glass and garnish with orange twist.

BMW
25 ml whiskey
25 ml Malibu rum
25 ml Baileys Irish Cream

Looking to give this famous liqueur a kick? Try this combination. Simply pour the ingredients over ice and stir well.

BOULEVARDIER
50 ml bourbon
25 ml Campari
25 ml sweet vermouth

Pair the bitterness of Campari and the rich sweetness of bourbon by stirring all 3 ingredients listed above in an iced shaker and stirring. Strain into a chilled cocktail glass with a small amount of cracked ice.

BURNING BUSH
50ml whisky
25ml runny honey
1 cinnamon stick
1 slice of fresh lemon
1 star anise
boiling water

Place the cinnamon stick, lemon and star anise in an Irish coffee glass with the whisky and honey. Top up with boiling water and stir well to infuse the flavours. This is a great cure-all cocktail for when you're feeling a little under the weather.

BUSHMILLS IRISH PUNCH

375ml water
225ml whisky
75ml runny honey
50ml Drambuie
50ml freshly squeezed lemon juice
8 tsps caster sugar
4 dashes of Angostura bitters
4 lemon slices
1 cinnamon stick

Put ingredients in a saucepan over a medium heat to warm through and stir frequently. Pour into a large punch bowl and let your guests help themselves. Serves approximately six people.

CARAMEL IRISH COFFEE

75ml fresh black coffee
25ml Baileys
25ml butterscotch schnapps
25ml whisky
caramel sauce
whipped cream

Every so often, somebody will take an already wonderful cocktail and somehow improve upon it. This fresh take on the Irish Coffee does just that, with the sweet tones of butterscotch and caramel cutting through the bitter black coffee. Build the drink into a warmed-through coffee glass and stir before topping with as much whipped cream and caramel as your heart desires.

CHERRY CREEK
50ml bourbon
25ml cherry liqueur
2 tsps fresh orange juice
2 tsps port
ice cubes

Shake ingredients well in your Savisto Boston Cocktail Shaker, strain into a cocktail glass and serve neat.

CREOLE
75ml bourbon
25ml sweet vermouth
a dash of Benedictine
a dash of maraschino liqueur
ice cubes
1 lemon twist (optional)

Stir the ingredients in a mixing glass over ice, strain into a chilled cocktail glass using your Savisto Hawthorne Strainer, garnish and serve.

DERBY
50 ml bourbon
25 ml sweet vermouth
25 ml orange curacao
25 ml fresh lime juice

Bring out the citrus notes in your favourite bourbon by shaking all the ingredients listed above with ice before straining into a chilled cocktail glass. Optionally add a lime garnish.

EL SALVADOR

50ml bourbon
25ml amaro liqueur
2 tsps crème de figue
2 tsps pimento dram
ice cubes
½ a fresh fig (optional)

Stir ingredients over ice in your Savisto Boston Mixing Glass, strain into a cocktail glass and serve neat with a fig slice for garnish.

EVERYBODY'S IRISH

50ml whisky
2 tsps crème de menthe
2 tsps green chartreuse
ice cubes

Shake ingredients well with ice, strain into a chilled cocktail glass and serve neat.

FALL FROM GRACE

50ml whisky
2 tsps cynar liqueur
2 tsps herbal liqueur
1 tsp Lillet Rouge
a few dashes of rhubarb bitters
ice cubes
1 orange twist (optional)

Stir ingredients well in a mixing glass until combined, then strain into a chilled cocktail glass. Garnish with orange twist and serve neat.

FRED COLLINS FIZZ

75 ml bourbon
10 ml simple syrup
Juice of 1 lemon
Dash orange curacao
200 ml lemonade

This is a very early variation of the original Tom Collins. It's made by pouring the bourbon, syrup and lemon juice into a cocktail shaker with ice and shaking well. Strain into a tall glass half-filled with crushed ice and add the curacao. Pour the lemonade into a collins glass and pour the rest of the ingredients on top.

FRISKY WHISKY

25ml fresh orange juice
25ml honey liqueur
25ml whisky
2 dashes of Angostura bitters
2 tsps caster sugar
ice cubes

Shake ingredients together with ice, strain into a chilled martini glass and serve.

GIANT'S GATE

50ml whisky
25ml Guinness
3 tsps caster sugar
2 tsps free range egg white
2 tsps freshly squeezed lime juice
cardamom pods

ice cubes

With its name an amalgamation of The Giant's Causeway and St. James' Gate in Northern Ireland and Dublin, respectively, this bitter, fresh and warming combination is a sure-fire crowd pleaser. Muddle a pinch of cardamom pods and combine with the whisky, Guinness, sugar, egg white and lime juice in your Savisto Boston Cocktail Shaker. Shake well, add a handful of ice cubes and shake again. Rinse a chilled cocktail glass with Guinness and strain the mixture in. Finish with another pinch of cardamom.

GREEN EYES

50ml double cream
25ml whisky
1 tsp crème de menthe
ice cubes

Shake ingredients well, strain into an Old Fashioned glass over ice and serve.

IRISH BLOND

50ml whisky
25ml curacao
1 tsp sherry
a dash of orange bitters
ice cubes
1 orange twist (optional)

Stir the whisky, curacao, sherry and bitters in your Savisto Boston Mixing Glass over ice then strain into a chilled cocktail glass. Garnish with orange twist and serve immediately.

IRISH COFFEE

120ml fresh black coffee
25ml double cream
25ml whisky
2 tsps demerara sugar

You'll be hard pressed to find a better combination than coffee and whisky. Packed with everything you need to see you through fatigue (provided you're not at work), it's said that your Irish Coffee should be as strong as a handshake. Brew up the coffee as you normally would, then pour it into a warmed-through coffee glass with the sugar and stir well. Add a shot of quality Irish whisky and top with cream before serving hot.

IRISH FARMHOUSE

50ml whisky
25ml fresh orange juice
4 tsps orange marmalade
2 tsps crème de cassis
2 dashes of Angostura bitters
a pinch of ground cinnamon
ginger ale
ice cubes
sparkling water
1 orange wedge (optional)

Thanks to the sweetness of the bramble liqueur cutting through the tart citrus flavour, the Irish Farmhouse is a perfectly balanced whisky highball. Shake the whisky, orange juice, marmalade, crème de cassis, Angostura bitters and cinnamon well with ice cubes until the marmalade is well mixed. Strain into a chilled highball glass over ice and top up with equal parts ginger ale and soda water. Garnish and serve.

JAMESON & GINGER

50ml whisky
ginger ale
ice cubes
1 maraschino cherry (optional)
1 wedge of lime (optional)

Fill a highball glass with ice, the whisky and top up with ginger ale. Squeeze the lime wedge over the drink then drop it in (along with the maraschino cherry) for garnish. Stir well and serve.

JOHN COLLINS

50ml bourbon
25ml freshly squeezed lemon juice
2 tsps caster sugar
club soda
ice cubes
1 maraschino cherry (optional)
1 wedge of fresh lemon (optional)

Stir the bourbon, lemon juice and sugar in a Collins glass on the rocks. Top up with club soda and garnish.

KOI COCKTAIL

50ml whisky
25ml TY-KU Citrus Liqueur
2 dashes of peach bitters
1 tsp freshly squeezed lemon juice
ice cubes
peach slices (optional)

If you've never seen TY-KU Citrus Liqueur in action before, you're in for a treat. The New York based company has been able to fashion the very first glow-in-the-dark liqueur which, when combined with these other vivid ingredients, creates an astonishingly beautiful mixed drink. Shake the whisky, liqueur, bitters and lemon juice well, then strain into a champagne flute. Garnish with peach slices and serve (in the dark).

LION'S TAIL

75 ml bourbon
50 ml allspice dram
25 ml lime juice
25 ml simple syrup
2 dashes Angostura bitters

Prohibition saw the exodus of a small army of top US bartenders to Europe – and this drink was created by one such London-based ex-pat. Place all the ingredients into a cocktail shaker with ice and shake well. Strain into a cocktail glass and serve.

LYNCHBURG LEMONADE

25ml bourbon
25ml freshly squeezed lemon juice
25ml triple sec
lemon & lime soda
crushed ice
1 slice of fresh lemon (optional)

Named after the town in Tennessee, home of Jack Daniel's Distillery, Lynchburg Lemonade is a straightforward and refreshing whisky sour that'll leave your taste buds tingling. Simply build the drink in a chilled jam jar over crushed ice, top up with lemon & lime soda and garnish with lemon slice.

MAMIE TAYLOR

75 ml whisky
50 ml lime juice
Ginger beer to top
Lime to garnish

This recipe dates back to the late 19th Century and was named in honour of Broadway actress, Mamie Taylor. If possible, opt for single malt scotch. Place a handful of ice cubes into a highball glass and add the scotch and lime juice. Top up with the ginger beer and garnish with a lime wedge.

MANHATTAN

50ml whiskey
2 dashes of Angostura bitters
2 tsps sweet vermouth
1 maraschino cherry (optional)

The first cocktail to introduce vermouth to the world of mixology, the Manhattan is one of the oldest and highly regarded cocktails on the market. Stir the ingredients with ice in your Savisto Boston Mixing Glass and strain into a chilled cocktail glass. Garnish with cherry and serve neat.

MASSEY COCKTAIL

25ml gin
25ml sweet vermouth
25ml whisky
1 tsp green chartreuse
½ tsp Campari
ice cubes
orange peel (optional)

Stir ingredients well over ice and strain into a chilled cocktail glass. Garnish with orange peel and serve.

MINT JULEP

75ml bourbon
2 tsps caster sugar
crushed ice
a sprig of fresh mint (plus extra for garnish)
1 wedge of fresh lemon (optional)

Muddle the mint and sugar at the bottom of a lowball glass. Toss in the bourbon, fill the glass with crushed ice and stir well. Garnish with lemon wedge, additional mint leaves and enjoy.

OLD FASHIONED

75ml bourbon
2 dashes of Angostura bitters
2 slices of fresh orange
2 tsps caster sugar
ice cubes
1 maraschino cherry (optional)

At the bottom of a traditional old fashioned glass, hydrate the sugar with the bitters. Muddle with orange slices, fill with ice and finally add the bourbon. Stir well, garnish with cherry and serve.

OLD MAPLE

50ml bourbon
2 tsps maple syrup
a dash of aromatic bitters
a pinch of ground cinnamon
ice cubes
orange peel (optional)

Build the drink over ice in a traditional old fashioned glass and stir gently. Garnish with orange peel and serve.

OLD THYME SOUR

50ml whisky
25ml freshly squeezed lemon juice
2 tsps caster sugar
2 tsps St Germain liqueur
1 tsp green chartreuse
1 free range egg white
a dash of Angostura bitters
a few sprigs of fresh thyme (optional)
1 lemon wedge (optional)

Coat half the thyme with the chartreuse in an old fashioned glass. Shake the remaining thyme with the whisky, lemon juice, sugar, St Germain, egg white and bitters until well mixed. Light the liqueur-soaked thyme and then strain the mix from the shaker over to extinguish. Garnish with a few more sprigs of thyme and lemon wedge.

PICKLEBACK

a shot of whisky
a shot of pickle juice

An odd trend that seems to be cropping up in bars of late, the Pickleback is simply a shot of whisky (usually Jameson's Irish whisky) followed by a shot of pickle brine. You'll have to try it for yourself to determine if it's worth the hype.

PRESBYTERIAN

50ml whiskey
club soda
ginger ale
ice cubes
1 lemon wedge (optional)

Fill a highball glass with ice, bourbon and equal parts ginger ale and soda. Stir, garnish and serve.

ROBERT BURNS

50ml scotch
25ml sweet vermouth
a dash of absinthe
a dash of orange bitters
ice cubes

Shake ingredients with ice and stir into a chilled cocktail glass.

SAZERAC

75ml whiskey
2 tsps caster sugar
a dash of Absinthe
a dash of Peychaud's bitters
1 lemon twist (optional)

Muddle the sugar and bitters before adding the whiskey and stirring thoroughly. You should be left with a syrupy whiskey. Meanwhile, rinse a chilled lowball glass with absinthe and dispose of the excess. Add the whiskey mixture to the glass, garnish with lemon and serve.

SCOTCH & SODA
50ml scotch
club soda
ice cubes

In a highball glass over ice, add the scotch and top up with soda.

SCOTCH MANHATTAN
50ml scotch
1 tsp sweet vermouth
a dash of Angostura bitters
ice cubes
1 maraschino cherry (optional)

Stir the ingredients over ice and strain into a chilled cocktail glass. Garnish with cherry and serve.

THE TULLY 10
50ml whisky
50ml hard apple cider
2 tsps caster sugar
2 tsps freshly squeezed lime juice
1 sprig of fresh mint
ice cubes
1 slice of fresh apple (optional)

Muddle two mint leaves with the sugar and add the whisky, cider and lime juice. Shake well with ice then strain into a highball glass on the rocks. Garnish with additional mint leaves and apple slice.

TULLY TEA
25ml freshly squeezed lemon juice
2 tsps caster sugar
2 tsps gin
2 tsps rum
2 tsps tequila
2 tsps whisky
cola
ice cubes

Shake lemon juice, sugar and all alcoholic elements together in your Savisto Boston Cocktail Shaker with ice. Strain into a highball glass over ice and top up with cola.

W&T
50ml whisky
tonic water
ice cubes
1 wedge of lemon (optional)

Like the humble G&T before it, simply pour the whisky in a highball glass over ice and top up with tonic. Garnish with lemon wedge and serve.

WARD EIGHT

50ml bourbon
3 tsps caster sugar
25ml freshly squeezed lemon juice
a dash of grenadine
ice cubes
1 maraschino cherry (optional)

Hailing from Boston, Massachusetts, the Ward Eight is a 20th century whisky sweet and sour. A quality rye whiskey will make a good substitute for the smoky bourbon, if you'd prefer. Fill your Savisto Boston Cocktail Shaker with ice and shake all the ingredients together well. Strain into a frosted collins glass, garnish with the maraschino cherry and serve on the rocks.

WHISKY BUCK

50ml whisky
ginger beer
1 tsp freshly squeezed lime juice
ice cubes
1 slice of fresh lime (optional)
1 maraschino cherry (optional)

Pour the whisky and lime juice over ice and top up with ginger beer. Garnish with cherry and lime and serve.

WHISKEY COBBLER

75ml whiskey
3 tsps caster sugar
club soda
crushed ice
2 lime wedges (optional)
1 mint sprig (optional)

Build the drink in a jam jar (filled with crushed ice) and stir well. Top up with club soda, leaving enough room for lime wedges, garnish and serve.

WHISKEY HIGHBALL

50ml whiskey
ginger ale
ice cubes

Pour the whiskey over ice in a chilled highball glass and top up with ginger ale.

WHISKEY SMASH

50ml bourbon
4 sprigs of fresh mint (plus extra for garnish)
1 tsp caster sugar
¼ of a fresh lemon (sliced)
ice cubes

Muddle the lemon and mint in your Savisto Boston Cocktail Shaker. Add sugar, bourbon and ice cubes and shake well to combine. Strain into a lowball glass on the rocks with additional lemon wedges and mint for garnish.

WHISKEY SOUR

50ml freshly squeezed lime juice
50ml whiskey
2 tsps caster sugar
ice cubes
1 maraschino cherry (garnish)

Shake ingredients well with ice cubes, strain into a chilled sour glass and garnish with cherry.

ZESTY IRISHMAN

25ml Drambuie
25ml whisky
1 tsp triple sec
ginger ale
juice of ½ a freshly squeezed lemon
ice cubes

Shake the Drambuie, whisky, triple sec and lemon juice with ice and strain into a lowball glass on the rocks. Top up with ginger ale and serve.

8. Beer

If the thought of a beer cocktail conjures up images of lager and lime (or even worse, 'snakebite'), it's time to put aside your prejudices. The fact is that fine ale has the strength and versatility to form the perfect base for a cocktail. What's more, when it comes to ales that are worth taking seriously, it just so happens that we're right in the middle of an artisan brewing revival – so there's plenty to experiment with.

With the exception of Guinness, when you're shopping for beers to create cocktails with, our top tip is to avoid the generic brands and head straight for the lesser-known labels. They are now becoming a staple of supermarket shelves and it's with the indie names that you're more likely to be rewarded with flavour and sheer quality.

Favourites for cocktails include Pilsner for refreshing clarity and Indian Pale Ale (IPA) for a darker hue and lots of different flavour notes, such as citrus and herbs. Wheat beer is similar to IPA but with a slightly smokier tone. At the other end of the spectrum lies stout with its dark and broody appearance and a flavour that's a match made in heaven with the likes of coffee and chocolate.

Finally, before you get to work, remember to have your Savisto Bostin Mixing Glass and Twisted Bar Spoon to hand. For obvious reasons, beer cocktails tend to be a shake-free zone.

BERLINER WEISSE MIT SCHUSS

330ml wheat beer
50 ml raspberry syrup

Whereas the British have a fondness for lager and lime, a popular German method of enjoying Weiss beer is to combine it with raspberry. Pour the shot of syrup into a beer glass first of all, then slowly pour the beer on top.

BLACK & TAN

½ pint pale ale
½ pint Guinness

Half fill a chilled pint glass with the pale ale, then float the Guinness over the top until glass is full.

BLACK VELVET

100ml stout
champagne

It's thought that this simple drink was created by the bartender of Brooks' Club in London in 1861 to mourn the death of Prince Albert. There are two ways of doing it: for a blended finish, half-fill a Champagne flute with stout, then simply top up with Champagne. If you prefer the liquids to remain largely separate, add the wine first, then pour the Guinness into the glass over an upturned spoon. This should cause the Guinness to run gently down the sides of the glass, resulting in a layered effect.

BOHEMIAN BAD ASS

75 ml dark ale or porter
100 ml Baileys Irish Cream
25 ml whiskey

For a rich and luxurious beer-based cocktail to savour, pour all the ingredients straight into a collins glass and stir before serving.

CAMPARI IPA

150ml IPA
25ml Campari
A splash of sparkling orange juice
1 orange peel (optional)

The ever-so-slightly fruity tang of IPA is a natural fit for Campari. For this beer-based spritzer, place a handful of ice cubes into a lowball glass and pour on the Campari. Top up with the IPA and add a splash of orange. To finish, rub a piece of orange peel around the rim of the glass before dropping it into the drink.

ESPRESSO STOUT

250ml stout
25ml coffee liqueur
2 shots of espresso

Make this well in advance of serving for best results. Allow your espresso to cool to room temperature and then pour it into a small jug along with the coffee liqueur (go for Kahlua for a flavour kick or Tia Maria for something slightly sweeter). Place in the fridge for at least 30 minutes or until it's well-chilled. Divide the stout between two half-pint pilsner or highball glasses. Slowly divide the expresso/liqueur mix evenly between the glasses. Stir and serve immediately. Serves two.

FRISBEE
50 ml cider
25 ml fresh blackcurrant juice
25 ml peach schnapps
lager

If you feel in the mood for giving your lager of choice a seriously fruity twist, this is the way to go. Pour the blackcurrant, cider and peach schnapps into a cocktail shaker with a good helping of ice and shake up. Strain into a highball glass and top up with the beer.

GINGER SHANDY
125ml wheat beer
2 tsps ginger wine
juice of two fresh lemons
ice cubes

Pour the lemon juice and ginger wine into an iced cocktail shaker. Shake well and strain into a cocktail glass. Top up the glass with wheat beer. For an extra gingery twist, garnish the glass with a matchstick of root ginger.

GUINNESS BLACK RUSSIAN

100ml stout
25ml coffee liqueur,
25ml vodka
100ml Coke
ice cubes
1 wedge of lime (optional)

This is a richer, sweeter twist on the traditional Black Russian, thanks to the addition of both Coke and Guinness. It also gives you that distinctive creamy head. Firstly, pour the coffee liqueur, vodka and Coke into a tall glass with 2 or 3 ice cubes. Stir gently to combine. Finally, top up with stout and serve with a wedge of lime.

GUINNESS MARTINI

100ml stout
50ml dark rum
25ml vodka
25ml crème de cacao
25ml cold espresso
ice cubes

Ideally, get hold of the dark variety of crème de cacao for this creamy Irish twist on the martini. This recipe will serve two people. Pour the rum into a mixing glass along with a handful of ice. Add the coffee, crème de cacao, vodka and stout and stir well. Strain into two martini glasses and serve.

HANGMAN'S BLOOD

330 ml bottle stout
50ml gin
50ml whisky
50ml rum
50ml port
50ml brandy
1 dash of champagne

Perhaps not the most elegant of concoctions, this cocktail nevertheless boasts an impressive literary endorsement. Anthony Burgess describes how it "induces a somehow metaphysical elation and rarely leaves a hangover. I recommend this for a quick, though expensive lift." Combine the spirits in a pint glass and then add the bottle of stout before topping up with champagne.

LAGERITA

25ml freshly squeezed lime juice
25ml tequila
25ml triple sec
bottle of Mexican beer

For a beer-based Margarita variation, season the rim of a lowball glass with lime and sea salt. Pour the tequila, triple sec and lime over ice in a cocktail shaker and shake well. Strain into a glass and top up with Mexican beer. Garnish with a lime wedge.

LAMBIC SANGRIA

750ml raspberry, cherry or peach beer
150ml Tequila
50ml Cointreau
juice of ½ a freshly squeezed lemon
3 peaches, stoned and sliced

Sangria is of course the go-to punch of the summer months and the traditional base is a bottle of cheap and cheerful red wine. For something a little sweeter, look out for Lambics, possibly the most wine-like beers on the market. Originating in Belgium, they tend to have an alcohol content higher than most other beers (which makes them a useful wine substitute). They tend to be available in fruit flavours such as cherry, peach and raspberry. Simply combine all the ingredients in a large jug. Feel free to experiment. Stir well and share with your guests.

MOJITO TECATE

330ml bottle light beer
25ml freshly lemon juice
25ml simple syrup
25ml white rum
a small bunch of fresh mint

Distinctive flavours have their place, but if it's smooth, refreshing drinking you want, it's hard to beat an everyday light beer. The absence of a strong aftertaste can also provide a handy neutral base for a cocktail. To give your beer something of a zesty kick without overtaking its smooth taste, this Mojito variation is worth a try. With your Savisto muddler, muddle the mint in a tall glass before adding the syrup, lemon juice, rum and beer. Shake gently and serve.

RASPBERRY BEER MOJITO

165ml beer
25ml spiced rum
half a fresh lime, chopped
1 small bunch of mint leaves
ice cubes

Add the lime and spiced rum to a highball glass and muddle them together using your Savisto muddling stick. Add 2 or 3 ice cubes and sprinkle in the mint leaves. Pour in the raspberry beer and, if you have them to hand, garnish with a couple of raspberries.

RED EYE

50ml tomato juice
beer
ice cubes
celery salt (optional)
1 wedge of fresh lemon (optional)
1 stick of celery (optional)

This is a variation of the drink that featured in the Tom Cruise movie Cocktail and is purportedly a cure for any hangover. We're not making any promises as to its pick-me-up qualities - but feel free to try it. Dump the tomato juice over ice into a pint glass rimmed with celery salt, top up with beer and garnish with lemon and celery.

SHANDYGRAFF

330ml cold beer or ale
330ml lemonade
1 sprig of fresh mint (optional)

A shandy need not be a tasteless sugary mess of a drink. Think in terms of quality and you can create a drink to be proud of. Combine your favourite lager with a traditional style lemonade in the same glass. Finish off with a sprig of mint and you have the perfect summer tipple.

SUMMER HOEDOWN

4 x 330ml bottles white beer
75ml maraschino liqueur
4 tsps caster sugar
1 seedless watermelon

For this refreshing beer-based punch, blend the water melon until liquefied. Strain the pulp to leave the liquid (you should have approximately 6 cups of juice). Pour into a serving jug and stir in the sugar. For best results, refrigerate for at least an hour. Just before serving, pour in the beer and liqueur and mix well.

SPIKED MICHELADA

330ml lager
2 tsps tequila
juice of a freshly squeezed lime
1 dash of Worcestershire sauce
2 tsps sea salt
ice cubes

You can buy ready-made concoctions of lager and tequila – but this is the real deal. Season a half-pint tankard, pilsner glass or highball glass by brushing the rim with lime juice. Tip the sea salt onto a plate and dip the rim of the glass into it to coat it. Pour a handful of ice cubes into the glass and add the tequila and remaining lime juice. Pour in your favourite lager. A splash of Worcestershire sauce and a slice of lime provide the perfect finishing touches.

THE STOUT DIPLOMAT

250ml chocolate or regular stout
50ml dark rum
25ml sherry

This cocktail was conjured up by a San Francisco restaurateur as a dessert replacement. If you can't get hold of chocolate-flavoured stout, try a dash of chocolate liqueur. Ideally, pre-chill all of the ingredients. Pour the rum and cherry into a long, straight glass and top up with stout. Stir gently, being careful not to disturb the head.

TENNESSEE TOM

25ml bourbon
25ml fresh orange juice
25ml runny honey
beer
ice cubes
lemon peel (optional)

Shake the bourbon, orange juice and honey will to create a strong syrup and pour this mixture into the bottom of a beer glass. Pour in the beer as you normally would, finishing with a good head. Garnish with lemon peel and serve.

WEISSEN SOUR

50ml white beer
50ml Bourbon
25ml freshly squeezed lemon juice
2 tsps caster sugar
2 dashes orange bitters
1 tsp orange marmalade
ice cubes
1 lemon twist (optional)

This whisky sour with an added beer kick is often attributed to San Francisco restaurateur, Kevin Diedrich. Combine all the ingredients in a shaker and shake very gently with ice. Add 3 ice cubes to a lowball glass and strain the ingredients into it. Garnish with a lemon twist.

If you've had any great deal of experience with cocktail making before now, you'll know that a number of them rely on liqueurs and cordials for depth of flavour. They're an essential aspect of mixology; introducing new cultural flavours to the more savvy consumer, but they can be (and are) so much more than that.

Although a cocktail – at least by its original definition – must include a spirit, sugar and a bitter, many have taken it upon themselves to mix up 'shooters,' which often use liqueurs as their flavour base. Shooters aren't designed to be savoured (in truth, some can taste awful), but rather to be knocked back quickly for an immediate buzz.

They don't all have binge drinking in mind, though, as bartenders around the world are starting to take their shooters very seriously indeed. They've almost become a potent bite-sized alternative to the cocktail in their own right; providing a quick, small burst of flavour much in the same way as the sample menu at a restaurant.

AFTER FIVE

2 tsps coffee liqueur
2 tsps cream liqueur
2 tsps peppermint schnapps

If you want a shot that goes down easily, you'll love the After Five. Alternatively known as the Girl Scout Cookie, this straight shooter gets straight to the point with a delectable combination of coffee cream and peppermint. Float the three ingredients on top of each other in a shot glass to create a perfect gradient, then knock it back and enjoy.

B-52

2 tsps coffee liqueur
2 tsps cream liqueur
2 tsps Grand Marnier

An ideal way to hone your floating skills, the B-52, not unlike the After Five, involves coffee and cream liqueurs but with the added citrus kick of Grand Marnier. Float the liqueurs one at a time in a shot glass and serve.

BAZOOKA JOE

2 tsps banana liqueur
2 tsps blue curacao
2 tsps cream liqueur
2 tsps freshly squeezed lime juice
ice cubes
1 lime wedge (optional)

Evoking memories of bubblegum from your youth, the Bazooka Joe is a sweet and fruity shooter that is guaranteed to boost feelings of nostalgia. Shake the ingredients well with ice in your Savisto Boston Cocktail Shaker, then strain into a shot glass. Garnish with a small lime wedge and kick it.

BEAM ME UP SCOTTY

2 tsps coffee liqueur
2 tsps banana liqueur
2 tsps cream liqueur

A warming shot for all you Trekkies out there, float the liqueurs into a shot glass in the order shown above and serve.

BLOW JOB

2 tsps amaretto
1 tsp cream liqueur
whipped cream

Yes, you read that name correctly. Though we wouldn't blame you for being sceptical; the Blow Job has been one of the most consistently popular shooters in recent times. Pour the amaretto and cream liqueur, in that order, in a shot glass and top with whipped cream. If you can get past the inevitably juvenile hysteria, the Blow Job will be one to add to your regular repertoire. If you want to follow a rather crude tradition, you're not allowed to use your hands to knock this back. A word to the wise – keep a napkin handy.

BUTTERY NIPPLE
25ml butterscotch liqueur
2 tsps cream liqueur

A sweet and indulgent shot that won't leave a sour taste in your mouth, simply float the cream liqueur on top of the butterscotch liqueur to create the Buttery Nipple.

CANDY CORN
1 tsp cream
1 tsp Galliano
1 tsp curacao

Perfect for dishing out at Halloween parties, there is a particular science behind a well-structured Candy Corn shot. It involves floating the ingredients in order of weight, which means Galliano first, then curacao and, finally, cream. This will create that autumn sunset effect that exhilarates the senses.

CEMENT MIXER
50ml cream liqueur
2 tsps freshly squeezed lime juice

Float the lime juice on top of the cream liqueur in a shot glass and consume straight away. Don't wait around too long, or this unusual combination will coagulate and become quite displeasing.

GLADIATOR

2 tsps amaretto
2 tsps Southern Comfort
lemon & lime soda
orange juice

Prepare a shot glass by filling with the amaretto and Southern Comfort, then half fill a lowball glass with the soda and juice. Drop the shot glass in and down in one.

GRAPE GRANSTAFF

1 tsp blackberry liqueur
1 tsp grape liqueur
1 tsp wilderberry liqueur
soda water
ice cubes

Mix the liqueurs together with a splash of soda water and ice cubes, strain into a shot glass and serve.

GRASSHOPPER

2 tsps crème de cacao
2 tsps crème de menthe
2 tsps single cream
ice cubes

A bite-sized version of the original Grasshopper cocktail, we've shrunk it right down to fit into a delicious single shot. Shake ingredients well with ice and strain into a shot glass.

IRISH FROG
25ml cream liqueur
25ml melon liqueur

An unusual combination perhaps, but the Irish Frog is a delightful little shooter not unlike the Fruity Irishman. Float the cream liqueur on top of the melon liqueur in a shot glass.

JAGER BOMB
50ml Jägermeister
red bull

Over the last number of years, the humble Jager Bomb has soared in popularity. Love them or hate them, you need to accept that there's just no avoiding the Jager Bomb anymore. Go out to any local watering hole and you'll see a group of young men and women sinking these anise-flavoured shooters, usually while screaming something about banter. The most common way of knocking these up are to drop a shot glass filled with Jägermeister into a highball glass and top up with Red Bull.

KOOL AID
2 tsps amaretto
2 tsps Midori
cranberry juice

Fill a highball glass with amaretto and Midori and top up with cranberry juice. Unlike other shooters, this can be treated more like a standard cocktail and served on the rocks (if desired) to be enjoyed thoroughly.

LIQUID COCAINE

25ml cinnamon schnapps
25ml Jägermeister
25ml peppermint schnapps
ice cubes

Not a drink you'll forget in a hurry, Liquid Cocaine has a rather unsavoury aftertaste, so you'll want a palette-cleansing chaser to accompany it. Shake the ingredients in your Savisto Boston Cocktail Shaker with ice and strain into a shot glass with your Savisto Hawthorne Strainer.

M&M

25ml amaretto
25ml coffee liqueur
ice cubes

Shake ingredients with ice and strain into a chilled shot glass.

NUTTY IRISHMAN

25ml cream liqueur
25ml Frangelico

Float the cream on top of the Frangelico in a chilled shot glass and serve.

OATMEAL COOKIE
25ml butterscotch schnapps
25ml cream liqueur
a dash of cinnamon schnapps
a dash of Jägermeister
ice cubes

Shake the ingredients well in your Savisto Boston Cocktail Shaker until the cream liqueur is well mixed with the rest of the ingredients. Strain into a shot glass and serve immediately.

ORGASM
2 tsps amaretto
2 tsps coffee liqueur
2 tsps cream liqueur
ice cubes

It might seem a little daunting asking your local bartender to give you an orgasm, but if you can get past the initial embarrassment then you'll definitely be left satisfied. Like a couple of shooters, the Orgasm is just a miniature version of its cocktail counterpart. Shake the ingredients until well mixed with ice and strain into a shot glass.

PBJ
25ml Frangelico
25ml raspberry liqueur
ice cubes

Shake the liqueurs well with ice and strain into a shot glass.

PEPPERMINT PATTY

25ml cream
2 tsps crème de cacao
2 tsps peppermint schnapps
ice cubes

Stir the ingredients over ice in your Savisto Boston Mixing Glass then strain into a shot glass.

POLAR BEAR

2 tsps clear crème de cacao
2 tsps peppermint schnapps
ice cubes

Fill your Savisto Boston Cocktail Shaker with ice, pour over the liqueurs and shake well. Strain into a shot glass with your Savisto Hawthorne Strainer and serve.

PROCRASTINATOR

25ml Frangelico
25ml honey liqueur
ice cubes

Pour the liqueurs over ice in your Savisto Cocktail Shaker and shake well before straining into a shot glass with your Savisto Hawthorne Strainer. This is a sweet and delicate shooter that will rival just about any carefully designed cocktail for taste. The combination of honey and nut is one that has been revisited for centuries, and it's easy to see why.

RED, WHITE & BLUE

2 tsps blue curacao
2 tsps grenadine
2 tsps peach schnapps OR 2 tsps vodka

There are two ways to create this 4th July inspired shooter. It's important to layer this in a certain order, which differs depending on whether you use schnapps or vodka. The method of floating is either grenadine, schnapps and curacao OR grenadine, curacao and vodka. Any other order and the density of the ingredients will desecrate this patriotic shot.

REDHEADED SLUT

50ml cranberry juice
25ml Jägermeister
25ml peach schnapps
ice cubes

One of the better ways to enjoy Jägermeister, as the bitter anise is well balanced by the fruit schnapps and cranberry juice. Shake ingredients well with ice and strain into an old fashioned glass using your Savisto Hawthorne Strainer.

SAMMY JAGER

25ml Jägermeister
25ml Sambuca
ice cubes

Created in tribute to the inferior of the two Van Halen frontmen, it won't take you long to figure out the reason for this unusual combination if you stare at the ingredients long enough. Speaking of ingredients; throw them together in your Savisto Boston Cocktail Shaker, shake well and strain into a shot glass using your Savisto Hawthorne Strainer.

SANTA SHOT

2 tsps crème de menthe
2 tsps grenadine
2 tsps peppermint schnapps

Float the ingredients on top of each other starting with the grenadine and finishing with the peppermint schnapps.

SCARLET O'HARA

50ml Southern Comfort
1 tsp freshly squeezed lime juice
cranberry juice
ice cubes
1 lime twist (optional)

Pour the lime juice and Southern Comfort over ice in a traditional Collins glass and top up with cranberry juice to taste. Garnish with lime twist and serve.

SLIPPERY NIPPLE

25ml cream liqueur
2 tsps sambuca

Pour the Sambuca over the cream liqueur in a shot glass and serve.

SMITH & KEARNS

50ml coffee liqueur
50ml double cream
club soda
ice cubes

Shake the liqueur and cream together with ice cubes and strain over fresh ice into a chilled lowball glass. Top up with club soda and serve.

SNAKEBITE

25ml runny honey
25ml whisky
2 tsps freshly squeezed lime juice
ice cubes

Shake the ingredients well with ice (until honey is well combined) in your Savisto Boston Cocktail Shaker. Strain into a shot glass using your Savisto Hawthorne Strainer and serve.

TOMAHAWK

50ml amaretto
2 tsps cinnamon schnapps

Build the ingredients in a shot glass and carefully stir to combine.

WOLF BITE

50ml fresh pineapple juice
25ml absinthe
25ml lemon & lime soda
25ml Midori
a dash of grenadine
ice cubes

Shake the ingredients (bar soda & grenadine) well with ice in your Savisto Boston Cocktail Shaker. Strain into a caballito glass and top with the soda and grenadine.

10. Champagne

If there's a celebration in the offing, you'll be keen to put on a show in the drinks department – but that's not to say you intend to spend the entire evening muddling, chopping and shaking in the kitchen. Enter the champagne cocktail: an instant sense of occasion and (for the most part at least) very little in the way of work.

For a purist, a champagne cocktail means it has to be champagne – but back in the real world the truth is that you don't have to invest in gallons of Brut to keep the party going. With a premier label, you are paying for that particular brand's distinct subtleties of flavour but once you blend the wine with a mixer, these subtleties are invariably altered. The upshot is that for the most part, it's perfectly acceptable to substitute champagne for the likes of Cava or Prosecco and save your Veuve Clicquot for the toast…

AXIS KISS

150 ml champagne
10 ml amaretto liqueur
10 ml crème de cassis

This sweet and fruity champagne cocktail comes with the other big advantage of being extremely easy to prepare. Simply pour the amaretto and crème de cassis into a chilled champagne flute before topping up with your champagne or sparkling wine of choice. The drink can be made drier or sweeter by reducing or increasing the amount of both liqueurs.

BELLINI MARTINI

Champagne of your choice
50 ml vodka
25 ml peach schnapps
3 raspberries for garnish

The original Bellini was made with white peaches, an ingredient that can be tough to source. This martini variation gives you the same look and feel with zero pureeing involved! Pour the vodka and peach schnapps into a cocktail shaker with a handful of ice cubes. Shake well before straining into a cocktail glass and garnishing with fresh raspberries.

BLOOD ORANGE BELLINI

150 ml champagne
30 ml freshly squeezed blood orange juice

Blood oranges may not have a flavour that's much different to regular oranges, but that distinctive red hue tends to be that little bit more effective as a head-turner compared to 'standard' orange. Simply pour the blood orange juice into a chilled champagne flute and top up the glass with champagne. Use a slice of blood orange as a garnish if required.

BLUE BELLINI

Champagne of your choice
50 ml peach schnapps
50 ml blue curacao

Here's a way of integrating blue curacao into your Bellini for a real eye-catcher along with a hint of bitterness. It could hardly be easier: start by pouring the peach schnapps into a champagne flute before 3/4 filling the glass with champagne. Finish off by adding the blue curacao and garnishing with a strawberry or cherry.

BLUSHING BRIDE

150 ml champagne
25 ml peach schnapps
25 ml grenadine

As well as having a pleasingly sweet blackcurrant flavour, grenadine also lends a vibrant crimson hue to a clear drink. In this case, it results in a blush-coloured champagne cocktail that's perfect for a wedding toast (hence its name) as well as being easy to scale up to cater for any large party. Pour the peach schnapps and grenadine into a flute and top up the glass with champagne.

BOURBON CHAMPAGNE COCKTAIL
150 ml champagne
50 ml bourbon whiskey
25 ml vanilla simple syrup

In terms of darker spirits that feature in champagne cocktails, brandy is by some way the most popular. As this recipe shows however, bourbon can work equally as well. To make the syrup, bring two cups of sugar and 1 cup of water to the boil. Split the vanilla beans lengthways in two and place in a heatproof jar. Pour the syrup over the vanilla beans and leave to stand for 8 to 10 hours. Pour the bourbon and syrup into a flute and top up with champagne.

BUCK'S FIZZ
50 ml champagne
100 ml orange juice

Taking its name from London's Buck's Club where it was conceived as an agreeable way to start drinking early in the day, the drink has now become something as a traditional part of Christmas Day breakfast in many households. It's also a favourite at wedding receptions. The exact proportions of champagne to orange aren't set in stone – but the classic recipe suggests combining 2 parts orange to one part champagne (go for freshly squeezed orange if possible).

CHAMPAGNE ANTOINE

150 ml champagne
25 ml gin
25 ml dry vermouth
10 ml Pernod
Lemon twist to garnish

If the Hemingway is a little too much to palate but you're a fan of that pastis flavour in your champagne cocktail, this could be the drink for you. Add the gin, vermouth and Pernod into a cocktail shaker filled with ice and shake well. Strain into a champagne flute and top up with champagne. Garnish with a twist of lemon.

CHAMPAGNE CASINO

150 ml champagne
25 ml Pernod
10 ml Cognac
1 brown sugar cube
Lemon twist for garnish

If you're more of a menthol than an Angostura Bitters person, this variation on the traditional Champagne Cocktail could be about to become your new favourite tipple. Start by placing the sugar cube in a champagne flute before gently pouring the Pernod over it (feel free to substitute Pernod for Absinthe if you prefer). Add champagne until the glass is almost full before floating the brandy on top. The lemon twist provides a finishing touch.

CHAMPAGNE COCKTAIL

Chilled champagne of your choice
100 ml cognac
2 dashes Angostura bitters
1 brown sugar cube

There are champagne cocktails – then there's the 'Champagne Cocktail', a classic grown-up treat that dates back to the mod-19th Century. Start by placing the sugar cube in the bottom of a chilled champagne flute. Add the bitters, then pour in the brandy and top up with champagne.

CHAMPAGNE FLIP

150 ml champagne
25 ml brandy
10 ml cream
10 ml simple syrup
1 egg yolk
2 dashes Cointreau
Pinch of nutmeg

This creamy and rich champagne recipe is created by pouring the brandy, Cointreau, cream, syrup and egg yolk into an ice-filled shaker. After shaking well, strain into a champagne flute. Fill with champagne and sprinkle with nutmeg.

CHAMPAGNE GRAND MARNIER COCKTAIL
(Recipe makes 6 drinks)
1 bottle champagne of your choice
150 ml Grand Marnier
100 ml lime juice
100 ml simple syrup

With its hint of pleasing sweetness, this blend is firmly within aperitif territory. Capable of being prepared very quickly (ideally just before serving), you add all the ingredients into a chilled jar. Stir carefully and gently so the champagne doesn't lose too much of its fizz before dividing between 6 champagne flutes. You can just as easily substitute champagne for any white sparkling wine.

CHAMPAGNE MARGARITA
150 ml champagne
25 ml tequila
10 ml Grand Marnier
10 ml lime juice
10 ml simple syrup

Shake all the ingredients apart from the champagne in an iced cocktail shaker and strain into a salt-rimmed cocktail glass. Top up with champagne and garnish with a slice of lime before serving immediately.

CHAMPAGNE PUNCH

2 bottles champagne
Juice of half a lime
2 tbsp caster sugar
Dash of Angostura bitters
250g raspberries

There's no absolute rules to dictate what you can and can't throw into your champagne punch – but here's a quick, easy and tasty version that you can use as a base to experiment with. Simply combine all the ingredients in a punch bowl and stir well, being careful not to mash up the raspberries. Add a good few handfuls of ice and serve up immediately.

CHAMPANSKA

150 ml champagne
50 ml vodka
50 ml lime cordial
Twist of lime for garnish

Vodka is the way to go for fortifying your champagne without overburdening it with strong flavours. For this sparkling taste of Russia, stir the vodka and lime cordial together in a mixing glass. Pour the champagne into a flute and carefully add the vodka and lime mix to the champagne.

CHATEAU CARDILLO

150 ml champagne
50 ml pear juice
Dash of black raspberry liqueur

Follow this recipe to add a gentle sweetness to your favourite champagne or sparkling wine. Simply pour the pear juice and raspberry liqueur into a chilled flute and top up gently with champagne.

CLASSIC BELLINI
150 ml champagne
50 ml peach juice, puree or nectar

This cocktail traces its roots back to mid-20th Century Venice where it was invented by the founder of Harry's Bar, Giuseppe Cipriani. Its Italian origins help to explain why Prosecco rather than champagne was the base of choice originally (it works equally as well with either). For authenticity's sake, try and get hold of flavoursome (and preferably white) peaches to puree. A single peach should give you enough puree for 2 to 3 drinks. Alternatively, opt for peach juice. Add the peach juice or purée to your champagne flute first of all before topping up with chilled champagne.

DEATH IN THE AFTERNOON
150 ml champagne
50 ml Absinthe

Not one for the faint-hearted, this cocktail was apparently the invention of Ernest Hemingway (its alternative name is the Hemingway Champagne). Try Pernod for a similar pastis taste but without the same level of potency. Pour the Absinthe (or Pernod) into a flute and top up with champagne. The end product is one of milky effervescence.

ELDERFLOWER CHAMPAGNE COCKTAIL

100 ml champagne
50 ml St. Germain Elderflower Liqueur
Soda water
Lemon twist for garnish

St Germain is a subtly fragrant elderflower liqueur that's ideal as an addition to a summery cocktail. For this drink, place 3 or 4 ice cubes in a chilled collins glass and pour in the liqueur, followed by the champagne. Top with soda water for extra fizz and stir well. Add the lemon twist before serving.

FESTIVE MIMOSA

Champagne of your choice
15 ml orange liqueur
75 ml fresh orange juice
1 tsp caster sugar

For this sweet and spicy twist on the classic Mimosa, start by seasoning your champagne flute. Do this by pouring the liqueur into a shallow bowl. Dip the rim of the glass into it before coating with the sugar to form a thin and sweet rim. Pour the remaining liqueur into the glass along with the orange. Top with champagne and serve straight away.

THE GHOST OF CHRISTMAS

Champagne (or sparkling wine) of your choice
3/4 cup of water
6 green tea bags
3/4 cup of honey
1 tbsp ground cinnamon
50 ml vodka
25 ml lemon juice
Fresh cranberries for garnish

Not a fan of mulled wine? This sweet and spicy festive treat takes a little work, but it's worth it. Firstly, prepare a honey and cinnamon syrup by allowing the green tea bags to steep in the warm water for 5 minutes. After removing the tea bags, stir in the honey and refrigerate the syrup until well chilled. Add the cinnamon before using. You should have enough syrup for about 12 drinks. For each cocktail, pour 25 ml of syrup along with the vodka and lemon juice into a collins glass. Top up with champagne or sparkling wine and garnish with cranberries.

HENNESSY BLACK APRICOT SUNRAY

(Recipe makes 1 large bowl of punch)
1 bottle champagne
375 ml cognac
750 ml apricot liqueur
300 ml apricot nectar
300 ml freshly squeezed lemon juice
1 ltr orange juice
4-6 sliced apricots
5 sliced lemons
1 sliced blood orange
12 brandied cherries

Fans of both Sangria and champagne punch should pay close attention to this rich party starter. Once you've got the peeling and slicing of fruit out of the way, creating it is a hassle-free process. Mix all the ingredients together in a large jug along with a generous handful of ice cubes. Stir well and serve.

KIR ROYALE
150 ml champagne
50 ml crème de cassis

The Kir is a traditional French cocktail combining blackcurrant with wine. The Kir Royale steps things up by replacing ordinary white wine with something a little more regal. Simply pour your crème de cassis into a chilled flute before topping up with champagne before serving immediately.

MIMOSA
75 ml champagne
75 ml fresh orange juice

The big difference between the French Mimosa and the British Buck's Fizz is the proportion of champagne to orange. When the amounts are equal, it's technically a Mimosa. Prepare either by pouring equal measures into individual glasses or mix in a pitcher.

NELSON'S BLOOD CHAMPAGNE COCKTAIL
150 ml champagne
25 ml ruby port
Dash of cognac

The body of the victor of Trafalgar was famously preserved in bottle of

French brandy for the return journey to England. This sparkling variation on the original 'Nelson's Blood' involves pouring the port into a flute before topping up with champagne. Finish off by adding a dash of cognac.

PEACH AND GIN CHAMPAGNE COCKTAIL
Champagne of your choice
25 ml gin
25 ml crème de peche

The enduring popularity of the classic Bellini demonstrates just how perfect a match there is between champagne and peach. As this cocktail demonstrates however, the Bellini isn't the only way to combine these two flavours. Here, simply pour the gin and crème de peche into a champagne flute and top with champagne for a dry, aromatic crowd-pleaser.

PIMM'S ROYALE
150 ml champagne
50 ml Pimm's No. 1

Cucumber, orange, strawberry and mint to garnish
As a rule of thumb, if a cocktail is suffixed by 'Royale', there's usually champagne involved and this sophisticated twist on Pimm's is equally at home in the beer garden and on the croquet lawn. To create it, combine the Pimm's and assorted flora in a long glass and muddle gently. Top up with champagne and a couple of ice cubes.

POINSETTIA

150 ml champagne
15 ml triple sec
50 ml cranberry juice

That ruby red tone coupled with the tang of cranberries help to make this the ideal aperitif before Christmas Day lunch. Start by measuring the triple sec into a chilled champagne flute before pouring in the cranberry juice. Top up with champagne.

QUEEN'S COUSIN

150 ml champagne
50 ml vodka
20 ml Grand Marnier
20 ml lime juice
1 tsp triple sec
Dash aromatic bitters

For a cocktail fit for distant royalty, pour the vodka, Grand Marnier, triple sec and lime juice into a champagne flute. Slowly pour in the champagne until it is almost full. Finally, add a couple of dashes of aromatic bitters.

RASPBERRY AND PEACH BELLINI

(Recipe makes 6 drinks)
Chilled champagne of your choice
1 punnet raspberries
4 peaches

For a fruity champagne-based treat, use a blender to puree the raspberries and peaches (remembering to peel the peaches beforehand). Combine these two purees and divide them between 6 chilled champagne flutes.

Top each glass with champagne and decorate with slices of peach if desired.

RASPBERRY CHAMPAGNE COCKTAIL

Champagne of your choice
50 ml raspberry liqueur (such as Chambord)
Between 2 and 4 raspberries.

Fans of the Kir Royale will appreciate this sparkly alternative. To begin, place the raspberries in the bottom of a chilled champagne flute. Pour in the raspberry liqueur and fill the glass with your champagne or sparkling wine of choice.

REGENT'S PUNCH

500 ml brandy
500 ml rum
500 ml Batavia Arack
500 ml blue curacao
3 cups hot green tea
3 cups lemon juice
3 cups orange simple syrup
1 bottle champagne
1 sliced pineapple
2 sliced oranges

For this classic champagne-based punch that dates back to the 19th Century, first make your orange syrup by bringing 2 1/2 cups of water and 100 ml of orange flower water to the boil. Add 3 cups of demerara sugar. Once its dissolved, remove the pan from the heat and allow to cool completely. To build the punch, pour the liquors, lemon juice, tea and syrup into a punch bowl and mix well. Before serving, add the champagne, sliced fruit and a couple of generous handfuls of ice.

SOUR WITCH

Champagne of your choice
50 ml absinthe
25 ml almond syrup
15 ml lime juice
3 or 4 pitted sour cherries
Grated nutmeg for garnish

This wickedly pungent champagne and absinthe cocktail is perfect for Halloween and works best with a dry champagne. To make, muddle the pitted cherries, lime juice and almond syrup in the bottom of a shaker. Add the absinthe with ice and shake well. Strain into a chilled flute and top with champagne. Finish with a grated nutmeg garnish.

STARLET

Champagne to top
50 ml absinthe
50 ml orange flavoured vodka
50 ml black raspberry liqueur
Raspberry to garnish

In this cocktail, the absinthe kick is tamed by the hint of orange and tones of raspberry. To create it, pour the absinthe, vodka and liqueur in a cocktail shaker filled with ice. Shake thoroughly before straining into a chilled cocktail glass. Top with champagne and garnish with a raspberry.

STOLI ACCOMPLICE

Champagne to top
50 ml vodka
25 ml simple syrup
15 ml fresh lemon juice
3 strawberries
Fine sugar for glass rim

Try and get hold of a great vodka (such as Stoli) and a dry champagne such as a brut or extra brut to really make this cocktail shine. To begin, use your Savisto muddler to muddle the strawberries and simple syrup in a cocktail shaker. Pour in the vodka and lemon juice and fill with ice before shaking well. Coat a cocktail glass with fine sugar and strain the contents of the shaker into it. Top up with champagne.

STRAWBERRY FLAPPER

(Recipe makes 2 drinks)
Champagne to top
8 fresh strawberries
4 dashes crème de cassis
10 ice cubes

For this strawberry-flavoured cousin of the classic Bellini, remove the leafy stem from each of the strawberries and place them in a blender along with the crème de cassis and ice cubes. Blend until smooth. Divide the mixture between flutes and top up each one with champagne.

217

THE SWEETEST THING

Champagne to top
50 ml bourbon (such as Maker's Mark)
25 ml crème de framboise
Raspberries for garnish

Here, the bourbon is softened by raspberry liqueur against a champagne backdrop to create a tipple that's perfect for Valentine's Day. It also happens to be extremely easy to create: simply pour the bourbon and crème de framboise into a champagne flute and top up with champagne.

VALENCIA ROYALE

Champagne to top
50 ml apricot brandy
25 ml fresh orange juice
3 dashes orange bitters
Orange twist for garnish

This fruity and delicious champagne cocktail dates back to the early part of the last century and it's the addition of orange bitters that gives it a distinctive tanginess. To create, pour the apricot brandy, orange juice and orange bitters into an iced cocktail shaker and shake up. Strain into a flute and top up with champagne.

WATERLOO SUNSET
Champagne to top
50 ml Beefeater 24 Gin
25 ml elderflower liqueur
10 ml raspberry liqueur

This cocktail was created in 2008 by Dan Warner, the then Beefeater Global Ambassador (hence the stipulation for Beefeater gin in the original recipe). In an iced cocktail shaker, stir up the gin and elderflower liqueur before straining into a champagne flute. Carefully pour in the champagne until the glass is almost full before adding the raspberry liqueur by pouring it over the back of a bar spoon for a layered effect.

WATERMELON FIZZ
(Recipe makes 6 drinks)
900g watermelon
250 ml champagne
2 tbsp lime juice
L tsp lime zest
2 tbsp mint to garnish
Hint of sugar syrup to taste

Unlike most champagne cocktails, this one takes plenty of planning – but the results are worth it. Put the watermelon in the fridge overnight. Chop it up, then process it in a blender along with the champagne, lime juice and zest until smooth. Depending on how sweet you want it, add up to a tablespoon of simple syrup. To serve, pour into 6 collins glasses and garnish with mint.

As with anything else, drinks have a tendency to drift in and out of fashion. Take wine-based cocktails for instance: they were incredibly popular in the early 1900s before taking a mid-century nosedive as the attentions of bartenders and punters alike shifted to the likes of gin, brandy and vodka (partly making up for lost time after the end of prohibition in the US). The likes of martinis are all well and good - but they are very much a pre or post-dinner drink rather than something you'd order to accompany food. One of the drivers behind the resurgence of wine cocktails over recent years has been the realisation that sometimes you want a drink with plenty of volume along with lots of flavour – especially if you're sitting down to dinner.

Champagne is often the go-to drink for mixologists looking to create something interesting - and we've put together a whole section on champagne-based cocktails. Here are the best of the rest...

RED WINE

BURGUNDY BISHOP
Red wine to top
50ml white rum
1/4 of a lemon
1 tsp powdered sugar

Rum and red wine are natural bedfellows when it comes to creating sheer depth of flavour as this classic red-wine based cocktail demonstrates. Pour the rum and powdered sugar into an iced cocktail shaker along with the squeezed juice from the lemon. Shake well before straining into a highball glass over 3 or 4 ice cubes. Fill your glass with red wine and decorate with chunks of whatever fruits you have to hand!

CACTUS BERRY
50 ml red wine
50 ml tequila
25 ml triple sec
10 ml sour mix
Splash lemon soda
Dash of lime juice for the drink (and a further dash for the rim)
Salt for the rim

This drink combines red wine and tequila in equal measure and is the perfect accompaniment to Mexican food. Wet the rim of a cocktail glass with lime juice and coat it in salt. Place all the ingredients in an iced-filled cocktail shaker. Shake before straining into the salted glass.

CARDINAL PUNCH

2 litres red wine
500 ml brandy
500 ml light rum
250 ml champagne
50 ml sweet vermouth
1 litre club soda
Juice of 12 lemons
Sugar to taste

For this zesty punch, stat by mixing lemon juice with sugar to take away some of its tartness (you can always add more sugar later on if it's still too sharp). Add the lemon juice to a punch bowl along with approx. 3 handfuls of ice cubes. Stir well before adding the rest of the ingredients. Stir again and garnish with whatever fruit you have to hand. Serves approximately 40 people.

FROTHY REDHEAD

1 scoop vanilla ice cream
75 ml club soda
75 ml red wine
1-3 tsp sugar

For this intriguing and refreshing combination of red wine and ice cream, place the scoop of ice cream in the bottom of a highball glass. Add the club soda followed by the red wine. (Don't shake it!). Add a sprinkle of sugar on top and serve immediately.

QUEEN CHARLOTTE

50 ml red wine
25 ml grenadine
Lemon lime soda

This elegant combination of red wine and grenadine is named after Charlotte Amalie, capital of the US Virgin Islands, which is itself named after the consort to the Danish King Christian V. Place 3 to 4 ice cubes into a collins glass and pour in the red wine and grenadine. Fill with soda and stir well before serving.

VAMPIRE VOODOO

50 ml red wine
50 ml gin
10 ml lemon juice
20 ml lime juice
Dash of red food colouring

This is the perfect cocktail to offer up to red wine fans at your next Halloween party and comes with the added benefit of being extremely quick and easy to make. Add all of the ingredients (apart from the food colouring) to an iced cocktail shaker and shake well. Splash in the food colouring before serving.

WHITE WINE

BONNIE PRINCE

50 ml gin
25 ml white wine
10 ml Drambuie

For this regal combination of gin and white wine with a hint of spice, simply pour all the ingredients into an iced cocktail and shake well. Strain into a lowball glass and serve with a couple of ice cubes.

HOLLYWOOD BOULEVARD

White wine
Soda water
25 ml vodka
50 ml fresh orange juice

For this orangey spritzer with a vodka kick, start off by lining the bottom of a highball glass with crushed ice before adding the vodka and orange. Stir well before adding white wine and soda to taste.

HOT SPRINGS

50 ml white wine
50 ml pineapple juice
1 ml Maraschino Liqueur
Dash orange bitters

A light cocktail in terms of alcohol content, the Hot Springs makes for relaxing summer drinking. To create, Simply pour all of the ingredients into a cocktail shaker with ice and shake thoroughly. Strain into a chilled cocktail glass and serve up immediately.

PINEAPPLE COOLER

50 ml white wine
50 ml pineapple juice
1/2 tsp powdered sugar
Soda water

For this Caribbean-inspired cooler, pour the wine, pineapple juice, powdered sugar and approx. 50 ml of soda water into a collins glass. Stir well. Add a healthy handful of ice cubes and top up the glass with soda water. Add a lemon peel and orange spiral to garnish.

WHITE SANGRIA

1 bottle white wine (such as Pinot Gris)
250 ml Grand Marnier
Handful of whole grapes
2 peaches, pitted and cut into wedges
Thinly sliced orange
Thinly sliced lime

As this tropical treat demonstrates, Sangria doesn't have to be made from red wine. To create, combine all the ingredients in a serving jug and refrigerate for at least 2 hours. Add 3 to 4 handfuls of ice before serving up.

FORTIFIED WINES

ABERDEEN FLIP

50 ml scotch whisky
30 ml sherry
1 egg
10 ml spice syrup
Dash chocolate bitters
1 tsp blackberry jam
Nutmeg

Place all ingredients apart from the nutmeg into your cocktail shaker and shake once (before you add the ice). Add ice then shake again. Strain into a lowball glass or a sherry glass and dust with grated nutmeg.

BARTENDER

15 ml gin
15 ml sherry
15 ml dry vermouth
15 ml Dubonnet Rouge
Dash Grand Marnier
Place all the ingredients into an iced shaker and shake well. Strain into a chilled cocktail glass.

LEMON SHERRY COCKTAIL

100 ml sherry
Juice of 1 lemon
Juice of half an orange
1 tsp honey

Place all the ingredients into an iced cocktail shaker. Shake well before straining into a highball glass. Use a slice of lemon or orange to garnish.

SAVOY SANGAREE

75ml sherry
1 tsp powdered sugar

Add the sugar and sherry into a lowball glass and stir. Garnish with orange or lemon peel and dust with nutmeg.

TV TOWER

50 ml grenadine
50 ml blue curacao
50 ml sherry

Starting with the grenadine and finishing with the sherry, layer the ingredients in a cocktail glass and serve.

PORT

ANTOINE'S LULLABY
25 ml dark rum
20 ml port
20 ml orange curacao
20 ml lemon juice

Stir (rather than shake) all the ingredients in a shaker or measuring flask before straining into a sugar-rimmed cocktail glass. Add a lemon twist as a garnish.

BROKEN SPUR
50 ml port
25 ml sweet vermouth
Dash triple sec

Stir all the ingredients in a mixing glass with ice. Strain into a cocktail glass and serve.

CHICAGO FIZZ
25 ml white rum
25 ml port
Juice of half a lemon
1 tsp powdered sugar
1 egg white
Club soda

Place all the ingredients apart from the club soda into an iced cocktail shaker and shake well. Place 2 ice cubes into a highball glass and strain the mixture into the glass. Fill with club soda and stir before serving.

CHOCOLATE PORT COCKTAIL

50 ml port
10 ml yellow chartreuse
1 tsp powdered sugar
1 tsp dark chocolate
1 egg white

Finely grate the chocolate and add it together with the rest of the ingredients into a cocktail shaker. Shake with ice and strain into a chilled cocktail glass.

CINZANO DEVIL

50 ml port
25 ml extra dry vermouth
1 dash of lemon juice

Pour the ingredients into a cocktail glass and stir well. For a garnish, add a slice of orange.

GIN SANGAREE

50 ml gin
20 ml port
1/2 tsp powdered sugar
1 tsp warm water
Soda water
Nutmeg

For this gin-soaked twist on the Savoy Sangaree, dissolve the powdered sugar in the water in the bottom of a mixing glass. Add the gin and stir. Place a couple of ice cubes into the bottom of a highball glass and pour in the combined water, sugar and gin. Part-fill the glass with soda water and stir. Float the port on top and sprinkle with nutmeg before serving.

JIM JONES

50 ml vodka
20 ml blue curacao
20 ml port
Dash of bitters

The port and blue curacao should combine in this drink to result in a deep purple colour. To prepare, pour all the ingredients into a cocktail glass and stir well.

LIL NAUE

50 ml brandy
25 ml apricot brandy
25 ml port
1 tsp powdered sugar
1 egg yolk

Pour all the ingredients into an iced cocktail shaker and shake well. Strain the ingredients into a red wine glass and sprinkle cinnamon on top before serving.

MONTANA

50 ml brandy
25 ml port
15 ml dry vermouth

Add a couple of ice cubes to a lowball glass. Add all the ingredients and stir well before serving.

PORT EGG NOG

50 ml port
1 egg
1 tsp sugar
Milk to fill
Nutmeg to garnish

Add the egg and port to an iced shaker and shake well. Strain into a tall glass and fill with milk. Garnish with nutmeg to serve.

PRESTO

50 ml port
50 ml brandy
50 ml blackberry brandy

For this fruity port and brandy combo, add all the ingredients to an iced cocktail shaker before straining into a cocktail glass.

PRINCETON

50 ml gin
25 ml port
Dash of orange bitters

This tangy gin concoction apparently originated in the Ivy league university that bears its name. To create it, pour all the ingredients into an iced shaker and shake well. Strain into a cocktail glass and garnish with a twist of lemon peel.

ST CHARLES PUNCH

100 ml port
50 ml brandy
25 ml triple sec
25 ml lemon juice
1 tsp sugar

Shake the brandy, triple sec, lemon juice and sugar in an iced shaker. Place a couple of ice cubes in a collins glass and strain the mixture on top. Float the port on top and garnish with a lemon slice.

TEMPTER
50 ml apricot brandy
50 ml port

Port is very much the unsung hero of cocktail ingredients: its luxurious texture and intense flavour make it an ideal accompaniment to fruity liqueurs. Here, port and brandy are combined in equal measure by stirring the ingredients together in an iced mixing glass before straining into a cocktail glass and serving.

12. Mocktails

Don't worry if you're not inclined to dabble with alcohol – we've got your back. Cocktails can be every bit as satisfying without alcohol, as the natural combinations of fruits are fantastic a way to keep refreshed in the summer or just when you fancy a more elegant drink at home. Packed with bold flavours and full of goodness, these Mocktail recipes have been carefully put together to deliver maximum pleasure under any circumstances.

These are no ordinary, hastily and thoughtlessly thrown together drinks; they'll rival any other cocktail you can find in this book for taste and appearance. In total honesty, you may find yourself pining after some of these gorgeous little drinks even when an alcoholic alternative is readily available. So, whether you've committed to Dry January or you're just trying to minimise your alcohol intake, there has never been a better time to volunteer yourself as the designated driver.

APRICOT GINGERINI

75ml apricot juice
75ml white grape juice
25ml ginger ale
¼ tsp ground cloves
ice cubes

Initially designed as a cure-all for the early stages of pregnancy, the Apricot Gingerini is a delicious mocktail with some serious health benefits. Shake the ingredients well with ice in your Savisto Boston Cocktail Shaker, strain into a martini glass and serve.

ARNOLD PALMER

75ml iced tea
75ml lemonade
1 slice of fresh lemon (optional)
ice cubes

Stir the ingredients together in a Collins glass on the rocks, garnish and serve.

AUTUMNAL TEMPTATIONS
75ml apricot juice
a dash of agave nectar
a dash of grapefruit juice
ginger ale
ice cubes

A stunning mixed drink to usher in the fall, Autumnal Temptations combines warm colours and flavours with sweet and sour fruit juices. The splash of grapefruit juice at the end gives this just a slight bitter edge that really kicks your taste buds into overdrive. Stir the apricot juice and agave nectar well in a Collins glass over ice until well combined; giving you a slightly syrupy consistency. Add a layer of grapefruit juice and top up with ginger ale before serving.

BABY BELLINI
50ml fresh peach juice
non-alcoholic pear cider

Build the drink slowly in a champagne flute and serve.

BEACH BLANKET BINGO
75ml cranberry juice
75ml grapefruit juice
soda water
ice cubes
1 lime wedge (optional)

Stir the juices together over ice in a chilled Collins glass, top up with soda water and garnish with lime wedge.

BERRY PATCH

180g frozen mixed berries
125ml whole milk
2 scoops of vanilla ice cream
a sprig of fresh mint (optional)

Blend the berries, milk and ice cream well until it reaches your desired consistency and pour into a chilled Collins glass. Garnish with fresh mint and serve.

BERRY SWEETHEART

75ml apple juice
75ml cranberry juice
25ml runny honey
ice cubes
1 fresh red cherry (optional)

Build the drink in a highball glass over ice and stir with your Savisto Twisted Bar Spoon. Garnish with cherry and serve.

CARDINAL PUNCH

50ml cranberry juice
25ml fresh orange juice
2 tsps freshly squeezed lemon juice
ginger ale
ice cubes
1 slice of fresh lemon (optional)

Pour the fruit juices over ice, top up with ginger ale and garnish with lemon slice.

CINDERELLA

25ml fresh orange juice
25ml fresh pineapple juice
25ml freshly squeezed lemon juice
a dash of grenadine
ginger ale
ice cubes
2 slices of fresh lemon (optional)

Shake the fruit juices in your Savisto Boston Cocktail Shaker to combine, then strain into a chilled Collins glass over ice. Top up with ginger ale, a splash of grenadine and garnish with lemon.

COCO COLADA

120ml fresh pineapple juice
50ml coconut cream
ice cubes
a sprig of fresh mint (optional)
1 fresh red cherry (optional)
1 wedge of fresh pineapple (optional)

Blend together the pineapple juice, coconut cream and ice cubes until it takes on a slush-like consistency. Pour into a chilled hurricane glass, garnish with mint, cherry and pineapple and serve with an umbrella on the side for complete authenticity.

CRANBERRY SPARKLER

75ml fresh cranberry juice
50ml ginger ale
non-alcoholic pear cider
ice cubes
a small handful of fresh cranberries (optional)

Stir the cranberry juice and ginger ale over ice in a chilled highball glass, top up with pear cider and garnish with fresh cranberries.

DALE EVANS

cola
juice of ½ a freshly squeezed lime
ice cubes
1 wedge of fresh lime (optional)

Pour the lime juice over ice in a chilled highball glass, top up with cola and stir well. Garnish with lime wedge and serve.

DOWN EAST DELIGHT

50ml cranberry juice
50ml grapefruit juice
25ml runny honey
orange juice
ice cubes

Stir the cranberry juice, grapefruit juice and honey over ice in a chilled old fashioned glass. Top up with orange juice and serve.

FLOSSY AUSSIE

75ml kiwi juice
50ml bitter lemon
2 tangerines (plus extra for garnish)
2 tsps caster sugar
2 tsps freshly squeezed lime juice
¼ of a sliced kiwifruit (plus extra for garnish)
ice cubes

Muddle the tangerines, kiwifruit, lime juice and sugar in your Savisto Boston Mixing Glass then add the kiwi juice and ice cubes. Shake well, then strain into a chilled martini glass and top up with bitter lemon. Garnish with additional skewered fruit and serve. You can substitute the tangerines for kumquats for a more authentic drink, but these can be hard to track down.

FROZEN GRAPEFRUIT SUNRISE

75ml fresh grapefruit juice
50g low fat yoghurt
2 fresh strawberries
1 tsp runny honey
½ a fresh banana
crushed ice

Blitz all ingredients until smooth, pour into a hurricane glass and serve.

GRAPE GLACIER

120ml grape juice
2 handfuls of seedless grapes (plus extra for garnish)
sparkling water
ice cubes

Blitz grapes, juice and ice cubes in a blender until smooth and pour into a chilled highball glass. Top up with sparkling water and stir well. Garnish with additional grapes and serve.

THE GREAT GAZOO

75ml fresh apple juice
25ml free range egg white
25ml freshly squeezed lime juice
2 tsps caster sugar
½ a fresh kiwifruit
a dash of aromatic bitters
a pinch of ground anise

Muddle the kiwi, sugar and anise in your Savisto Boston Cocktail Shaker, then add the apple juice, egg white, lime juice and bitters. Shake well to combine, strain into a cocktail glass and serve.

GREEN LEMONADE

110ml lemonade
50ml freshly squeezed lime juice
4 slices of fresh kiwifruit (plus extra for garnish)
3 tsps caster sugar
ice cubes

Muddle the kiwifruit and sugar in your Savisto Boston Cocktail Shaker and add the ice, lemonade and lime juice. Shake well to combine, then strain over ice in a chilled highball glass. Garnish with additional slices of kiwifruit.

KEY LIME COCONUT

75ml lime soda
25ml coconut milk
25ml freshly squeezed lime juice
ice cubes
1 tsp caster sugar
1 tsp vanilla extract
1 tsp desiccated coconut (optional)
1 wedge of fresh orange (optional)
a handful of fresh mixed berries (optional)

Shake the lime juice and soda, coconut milk, caster sugar and vanilla extract well and strain into a chilled martini glass using your Savisto Hawthorne Strainer. Garnish with desiccated coconut, orange wedge and a handful of fresh berries.

MANGO JULIUS

120ml fresh mango juice
50ml whole milk
2 tsps caster sugar
1 scoop of vanilla ice cream
1 tsp vanilla extract
ice cubes

Blend all ingredients well and pour into a chilled hurricane glass.

MOCKITO

50ml pomegranate juice
2 tsps caster sugar
½ a fresh sliced lime
a small bunch of fresh mint (plus extra for garnish)
lemonade
ice cubes
a handful of pomegranate seeds (optional)
1 wedge of fresh lime (optional)

We're going to be straight with you, this alcohol-free Mojito is arguably better than the real version. The fresh, refreshing flavours of mint, lime and pomegranate burst through the bitter lemon to create a sensation quite unlike any other. To begin, muddle the sugar, lime and mint in the bottom of a chilled highball glass. Top up with a handful of ice cubes, the pomegranate juice and as much lemonade as you like. Drop a handful of pomegranate seeds into the mix along with some fresh mint leaves and a wedge of lime to finish off this unbelievable mixed drink.

NOT TODDY

2 tsps runny honey
1 tsp freshly squeezed lemon juice
a pinch of cinnamon
a pinch of cloves
a pinch of nutmeg
freshly brewed tea
1 cinnamon stick (optional)
1 slice of fresh lemon (optional)

Combine the honey, lemon juice and spices in the bottom of an Irish coffee glass, top up with hot tea and stir well until the honey and spices are well mixed into the liquid. Garnish with lemon and cinnamon stick and serve immediately.

ORANGE JULIUS

120ml fresh orange juice
50ml whole milk
2 tsps caster sugar
1 scoop of vanilla ice cream
1 tsp vanilla extract
ice cubes
runny honey (optional)
1 slice of fresh orange (optional)

Blend the milk, sugar, ice cream, vanilla extract, orange juice and ice cubes until smooth. Add more orange juice if the mixture is too thick for your liking, or more ice if it's too thin. Squeeze some honey around the outside of a chilled hurricane glass, then pour in the blended mixture. Garnish with orange slice and serve.

PEACH JULIUS
120ml fresh peach juice
50ml whole milk
2 tsps caster sugar
1 scoop vanilla ice cream
1 tsp vanilla extract
ice cubes
1 wedge of fresh peach (optional)

Blend the ingredients well until smooth. Pour into a chilled hurricane glass, garnish with peach wedge and serve.

PEACH SUNRISE
75ml fresh peach juice
25ml grenadine
lemon & lime soda
ice cubes

The younger (and sober) sibling of the sunrise family of cocktails, the Peach Sunrise is a delightful little fruity thirst-quencher ideal for the summertime. Fill a lowball glass with ice and pour in the peach juice. Top up with soda and carefully pour in the grenadine. It should sink to the bottom and create the sunrise effect before settling into the drink.

PILGRIM'S PUNCH
75ml cranberry juice
75ml grape juice
sparkling water
ice cubes
freshly cracked black pepper

Pour the fruit juices over ice cubes in a chilled highball glass. Top up with sparkling water and finish with a pinch of cracked black pepper for a warming kick through the sweet juices.

PREGNANT PROVENCE
75ml ginger ale
50ml lemonade
2 tsps caster sugar
2 tsps freshly grated lemon zest
a handful of fresh white grapes
a pinch of lavender petals
a sprig of fresh rosemary (plus extra for garnish)

In your Savisto Boston Mixing Glass, muddle together the rosemary, grapes, sugar, lavender and lemon zest. Top up with lemonade and ice cubes, then shake well and strain into a chilled cocktail glass. Finish with ginger ale and garnish with a small sprig of rosemary.

PUSSYFOOT

50ml freshly squeezed lime juice
25ml freshly squeezed lemon juice
1 free range egg yolk
fresh orange juice
sparkling water
ice cubes

Shake the lemon, lime, sugar and egg yolk well in your Savisto Boston Cocktail Shaker until egg is fully dissolved. Strain into a chilled Collins glass, top up with equal parts orange juice and sparkling water and serve on the rocks.

RASPBERRY JULIUS

200g fresh raspberries (plus extra for garnish)
50ml whole milk
2 tsps caster sugar
1 scoop of vanilla ice cream
1 tsp vanilla extract
ice cubes

Blend ingredients together with ice and pour into a chilled hurricane glass.

RENO COCKTAIL

50ml fresh grapefruit juice
25ml freshly squeezed lime juice
2 tsps grenadine
1 tsp caster sugar
ice cubes
1 orange twist (optional)

Shake ingredients well with ice cubes and strain into a chilled cocktail glass. Garnish with orange twist and serve.

ROOT BEER FLOAT

root beer
vanilla ice cream

Fill a coffee glass with root beer until ¾ full, then drop in a scoop of vanilla ice cream. Keep some kitchen towels at hand to mop up any spillages.

ROY ROGERS

1 tsp grenadine
cola
ice cubes
1 fresh orange wedge (optional)
1 fresh red cherry (optional)

As close to a Cherry Coke as you'll get yourself, the Roy Rogers is a delicious (but somewhat naughty) drink to enjoy every so often. Pour the cola and grenadine over ice in a chilled Collins glass and stir well to combine the flavours. Garnish with orange and cherry and serve.

SHIRLEY TEMPLE

75ml ginger ale
75ml lemon & lime soda
a dash of grenadine
ice cubes
1 maraschino cherry (optional)

Pour the sodas over in in a chilled Collins glass, add the grenadine and stir well to combine. Garnish with maraschino cherry and serve.

SPRING FEVER

50ml fresh apple juice
50ml fresh orange juice
25ml freshly squeezed lemon juice
25ml mango syrup
ice cubes
1 wedge of fresh orange (optional)

Shake the juices and mango syrup well with ice and strain into a Collins glass on the rocks. Garnish with orange wedge and serve.

STRAWBERRY LEMONADE

75ml sparkling water.
50ml freshly squeezed lemon juice
4 sliced strawberries (plus extra for garnish)
3 tsps caster sugar
ice cubes

Muddle the strawberries and sugar in your Savisto Boston Cocktail Shaker and add the ice, lemon juice and water. Shake well, strain into a Collins glass on the rocks and garnish before serving. If you aren't a fan of strawberries (but why wouldn't you be?) you can substitute them for other seasonal fruit.

SUNDOWNER

grape juice
sparkling water
ice cubes
a sprig of fresh mint (optional)

Pour two parts grape juice to one part water into a white wine glass over ice and stir well. Garnish with sprig of mint, and serve for a perfect alcohol-free alternative to white wine or champagne.

VIRGIN MARY

75ml tomato juice
2 tsps freshly squeezed lime juice
a dash of tabasco sauce
a dash of Worcestershire sauce
a pinch of celery salt
a pinch of freshly ground black pepper
ice cubes
1 celery stalk (optional)
1 slice of cucumber (optional)

Pour the tomato juice, lime juice, tabasco sauce and Worcestershire sauce in a highball glass over ice. Add the celery salt and black pepper and stir well. Garnish with celery stalk and cucumber slice and serve.

VIRGIN SUNRISE

2 tsps grenadine
orange juice
ice cubes
1 orange twist (optional)
1 fresh red cherry (optional)

A sober Tequila Sunrise, this gorgeous mixed drink is perfect for with a late breakfast to invoke feelings of vacation brunches on sunlit balconies. Fill a highball glass with ice cubes and orange juice, then slowly add the grenadine to create the sunrise. It should sink to the bottom before eventually settling towards the top as you drink. Garnish with orange and cherry and serve.

VIRGINIA PUNCH

50ml cranberry juice
50ml pomegranate juice
2 tsps caster sugar
2 tsps freshly squeezed lime juice
non-alcoholic apple cider
ice cubes
2 fresh cranberries (optional)
1 wedge of fresh apple (optional)

Shake the sugar and fruit juices together with ice cubes in your Savisto Boston Cocktail Shaker. Strain over ice in a chilled highball glass, top up with cider and garnish with apple and cranberries.

GLOSSARY

We know the world of cocktails can be daunting and overwhelming for fledgling enthusiasts, so we thought you'd appreciate some clarification on some of the more common bartending jargon.

By no means should this be considered a definitive list, but here you'll find most of the terminology that you're likely to stumble across - and subsequently raise an eyebrow at - for your convenience.

ABSINTHE
An anise-flavoured and highly potent distilled spirit derived from botanicals and herbs.

AGE
How long a spirit has been stored.

AMARETTO
A sweet almond liqueur.

APERITIF
A term used to describe a before-dinner cocktail, designed to stimulate the appetite.

BAR SPOON
A perforated spoon with a long, twisted handle.

BASE
The primary ingredient, usually a spirit, of a cocktail.

BITTERS
A liquor, often flavoured with fruit and herbs, typically used in very small amounts as a flavouring for cocktails.

BLITZ
The act of pulsing something in a blender.

BUILD
To mix a drink in the same glass it is intended to be consumed from.

CALVADOS

Glossary

An aged French brandy comprised of up to forty-eight different varieties of apple.

CHILL

To prepare a cocktail glass as required by leaving it in the freezer for at least a couple of hours before use.

COBBLER

A cocktail which combines a liqueur with fruit juice, sugar and ice.

CURACAO

An orange liqueur, flavoured with the peel of bitter oranges in the Caribbean.

DASH

An approximate measure, no more than a few drops.

DIRTY

When a traditional cocktail is changed by adding a small amount of another ingredient (i.e. olive brine) that alters the colour or taste.

DRY

The absence of vermouth in a Martini.

FLAME

The act of lighting fruit peel over a cocktail in order to extract its essential oils.

FLOAT

The act of layering ingredients 'over' one another to create a gradient effect.

FROZEN

A drink that is blended with ice or frozen fruit.

GARNISH

The decorative aspect of a cocktail, often fruit or herbs.

GRENADINE

A common tart and sweet bar syrup with a deep red colour, derived from pomegranate.

HIGHBALL

A cocktail served in a Highball glass.

LIQUEUR

A sweet spirit combined with a natural flavour from fruit, plants or nuts.

MARASCHINO

A liqueur derived from the distilled cherries of the Marasca tree.

MIXER

The non-alcoholic element of a mixed drink.

MUDDLE

The act of grinding or pressing to extract juice or mash ingredients together.

NEAT

A drink served without ice cubes.

ON THE ROCKS

A drink served over ice.

RIM

The act of coating the edge of a cocktail glass with juice, sugar, salt or a combination.

SCHNAPPS

A sweet spirit from Europe, usually flavoured with fruit such as peach or apple.

SHAKE

The act of shaking ingredients and ice together in order to rapidly chill your drink.

SIMPLE SYRUP

The result of boiling water and sugar into a clear syrup used to sweeten some cocktails.

SLOE GIN

A red liqueur made by infusing gin with sloe berries and sugar.

STIR

A method of mixing ingredients together with ice without diluting its contents.

STRAIN

The act of straining your cocktail to remove unwanted bits of ice or fruit pulp.

TRIPLE SEC

A variety of the Curacao liqueur.

TOP SHELF

The best quality spirits.

TWIST

A long piece of citrus peel that has been twisted to extract oils and decorate.

VERMOUTH

A fortified wine flavoured with botanicals and available in either dry or sweet varieties.

ZEST

The aromatic fragrance of citrus fruits.

COCKTAIL INDEX

Index

More products from our range available at **www.savisto.com**

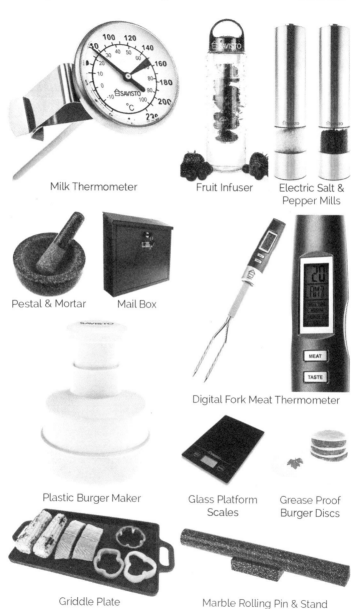

Milk Thermometer

Fruit Infuser

Electric Salt & Pepper Mills

Pestal & Mortar

Mail Box

Digital Fork Meat Thermometer

Plastic Burger Maker

Glass Platform Scales

Grease Proof Burger Discs

Griddle Plate

Marble Rolling Pin & Stand

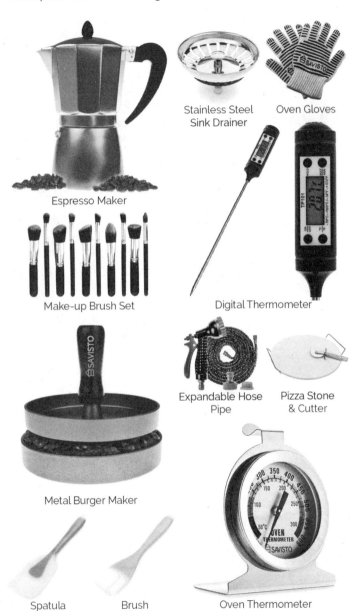

Espresso Maker

Stainless Steel
Sink Drainer

Oven Gloves

Make-up Brush Set

Digital Thermometer

Metal Burger Maker

Expandable Hose
Pipe

Pizza Stone
& Cutter

Spatula

Brush

Oven Thermometer